HOME THOUGHTS
FROM ABROAD

HOME THOUGHTS FROM ABROAD

Distant Visions of Israel in
Contemporary Hebrew Fiction

RISA DOMB

VALLENTINE MITCHELL
LONDON

First published in 1995 in Great Britain by
VALLENTINE MITCHELL & CO. LTD.
Newbury House, 900 Eastern Avenue,
London IG2 7HH

and in the United States of America by
VALLENTINE MITCHELL
c/o ISBS
5804 N.E. Hassalo Street, Portland, Oregon 97213–3644

British Library Cataloguing in Publication Data

Domb, Risa
Home Thoughts from Abroad: Distant
Visions of Israel in Contemporary Hebrew
Fiction
I. Title
892.43609

ISBN 0 85303 303 X (cloth)
ISBN 0 85303 304 8 (paper)

Library of Congress Cataloging-in-Publication Data

Domb, Risa.
    Home thoughts from abroad : distant visions of Israel in
contemporary Hebrew fiction/Risa Domb.
        p. cm.
    Includes bibliographical references and index.
    ISBN 0-85303-303-X (cloth)— ISBN 0-85303-304-8 (pbk.)
    1. Israeli fiction—History and criticism. 2. Expatriation in
literature. 3. Europe—In literature. 4. Israel—In literature.
I. Title.
PJ5030.E94D66   1995
892.4'3609—dc20   95-2681
                                                          CIP

Printed in Great Britain by
Bookcraft (Bath) Ltd, Midsomer Norton, Avon

For my daughter, Tamar

Contents

Introduction

People travel far to
say: this reminds me of another place.

Yehuda Amichai[1]

What do all those who leave their homes and pick themselves up to wander from place to place see? It might be a
primeval law, or a mocking imagination: as the ancient
proverb says, your happiness lies thence where you are
not.

S. Y. Agnon[2]

The major waves of Jewish Immigration from Europe to pre-
sent-day Israel during the late nineteenth century and most of
the first half of the twentieth century culminated in the establishment of the State of Israel in 1948. The geographical shift
of Jewish existence from west to east entailed a shift from an
existence outside time and space to an existence within space.
From that time onwards a dialectical tension existed between
Israel and Europe, between home and abroad. 'Home' in this
context is defined by the national boundaries of Israel, and
'abroad', for the historical reasons mentioned, is Europe. Both
concepts of home and abroad are related to the concept of
place.

The tension between the alternatives of home and abroad
can be seen as a tension between 'inside' and 'outside', to bor-
row the French phenomenologist Gaston Bachelard's terminology,[3] or 'home' and 'horizon' to use Robert Alter's.[4] Bachelard
observed that inside and outside form a dialectic of division,
and that beyond their formal opposition lie alienation and hostility. Yet, they are always ready to be reversed, to exchange
their hostility. He postulates that inside and outside are not
abandoned to their geometrical opposition and that human
beings are composed of both. This being the case, the border or
distinction between these two oppositions is ambiguous. Alter's
concepts of 'home' and 'horizon' are also inherently unstable,

1

and they too determine the make-up of individual human beings, and that of a nation. National concerns have traditionally been the principal locus of the imaginative work of Hebrew writers. But, finding the geographical and cultural limits to their fictional worlds constricting, many Israeli writers strove to escape by maintaining connections against all the odds with the outside world, with the horizon. At times they even wondered if life might not be more fully lived somewhere else, creating a tension between homeland and horizon. In fact, this oscillation between Europe and the attempt to recover the Israeli self by recapitulating the world of the writers' childhood marks contemporary Israeli literature. Alter suggests the tension reflects

> the key psychological paradox of an imaginative literature that feels itself to be a full participant in modern culture at large, and yet is boxed into a tiny corner of geography, linguistically limited to at most a scant two million readers. In this regard, contemporary Hebrew literature provides a vivid if extreme paradigm for the difficult fate of all small cultures in an age of vast linguistic-cultural blocs and of global communications.[5]

This fate is not new in the development of Hebrew literature. Alan Mintz noted that the inside/outside dichotomy introduced an important thematic opposition during the Jewish Age of Enlightenment: '"inside/outside" would automatically be taken as relating to the conflict between Jewish values and secular European values, between what lay inside the "camp" or the "home" and what lay beyond it.'[6]

One of the most striking facts of modern Hebrew literature is that it arose in Europe. It modelled itself on European cultural and literary traditions as well as on its own rich Jewish literary sources. Consequently, Hebrew writers could draw inspiration from their surrounding intellectual environment even after they had moved away from Europe. However, attitudes towards Europe changed after disappointment with the Europeanisation of Hebrew culture that came with the Enlightenment, which at its extreme led to assimilation. Although still keeping up with European literary genres, the literature of the first Hebrew writers in Israel, in the 1940s and early 1950s, became insular and regional. In Hegelian terms of action and reaction, it is not surprising to discover that the writers who followed, the 'New Wave' of the mid-1950s and 1960s, reacted against their predecessors and turned away from regionality towards universalism. They felt that the actual geographical limits to the fictional world restricted the imagination of their predecessors. Once again, Hebrew literature looked outwards, towards Europe. This shift coincided with the political and economic circumstances which enabled Israeli writers to travel abroad more easily. However, one has to be cautious not to over-emphasise this factor, but rather to consider both the internal and external forces that brought about this change. David Lodge has remarked, concerning similar considerations, that: 'The process cannot be accounted for by reference to fortuitous external circumstances alone, but must have some cause within the system of literature itself.'[7]

Bearing all this in mind, it is not surprising that from the 1970s onwards in many contemporary novels Israeli protagonists travel abroad, away from the spatial narrowness of their existence at home. As Angela Ingram has said: 'Geographical exile is often more a *getting away from* than *going to* a place. This is probably true in varying degrees for most exiles, expatriates, leavers of countries.'[8] The flight of the Israeli protagonists is indeed similar in some respects to expatriatism. Both flights can serve as geographic metaphors for psychic states of mind and for the search for self-identity, as Susan Willis has written: 'The notion of travelling through space is integral to the unfolding of history and the development of the individual's consciousness with regard to the past. The voyage over geographic space is an expanded metaphor for the process of one person's coming to know who she is.'[9] Expatriatism, like travel, provides freedom of mind and spirit from convention, from pressure to conform. It is a flight from home and alienation from a conventional destiny. Furthermore, Gabriel Josipovici has noted, two of the great thinkers of our modern age, Kafka and Benjamin, regarded exile only in positive terms:

They are our two greatest spokesmen for the distinctively modern in modern art because they both recognize that it is an art of exile and that there is no fatherland to which to return. This looks like a gloomy position but in fact it is oddly positive. . . . What . . . Benjamin would argue is that exile, lack of fullness, lack of rootedness, is man's essential condition, and that what modern art does is to help him to understand that condition and rejoice in it.[10]

In this era of upheaval, many authors outside Hebrew literature are also writing about the idea of displacement. Travelling into a different locus is similar also to the travel undertaken by the protagonists of the 1990s' 'New Fiction' in France. Common to all New Fictionists is their desire to deviate from the real world into a parallel universe, disquietingly similar to, or different from, our own. Their scepticism about claims to act freely and wilfully in the world induces them to bring their characters into contact with other-worldly forces. 'The typical hero of a New Fiction tale sets out on a quest during which he is gradually enlightened about the meaning of his life, initiated into some corpus of esoteric knowledge, or brought to a vista from which he catches a glimmer of some inaccessible mythical truth.'[11] By contrast, Israeli writers do not necessarily place their characters in a metaphysical world, and whereas New Fictionists only rarely acknowledge the emotions as an integral element of human nature, Israeli writers dwell on them.

In this study, I am not concerned with protagonists who are expatriates, but rather with those who leave and then return, and with novels where the tension between home and abroad is manifested in the dialectics of inside and outside.[12] This movement between two distinct territories provides the writers with the opportunity to use place as an important literary device, on both the thematic and structural levels of the text.

The travelogue had been the most common genre of early Hebrew writing of the turn of the century in Palestine, disseminating information about and propaganda for life there. Through the travels away from home yet within the Holy Land, the overt aim, ironically enough, had been to convey a sense of belonging to the one and only place.[13] However, from the middle of the 1950s Hebrew literature assumed a new dimension and the dominant oscillation became that between home and abroad, rather than home and away, as Gershon Shaked has pointed out:

> The Exile was no longer abhorred and negated. It ceased being a source of nightmare or an object of nostalgia and instead it became a source of attraction and magic; no longer an old world, which is remembered only in positive terms, and no longer an enigma. But, rather a wonderful and open world seductive with its magic. . . the protagonists of the '50's and the '60's were amazed by the strangeness of the world, its openness and the unlimited possibilities of expanse and freedom on the one hand, and the negative and demonic forces awaiting the Jew and the Israeli in this strange world, on the other.[14]

Ironically, the much desired outside or horizon of the early Hebrew writers of the Age of Enlightenment had now become analogous to exile.

Thus, the renewed encounter with Europe triggers admiration and attraction as well as hostility and repulsion. Some protagonists escape to Europe and others from Europe, but in both cases Europe never serves as just a tourist's sightseeing region abroad but as a world which stands in total contrast to Israel. On the whole, the initial reaction to Europe is one of wonder at its magic. Amnon Rubinstein has pointed out that to the Israeli, going abroad is a flight

> from the compression and the tension to the wider world where one can, all of a sudden, shed all the pressures of life in a compressed hothouse; one can be anonymous, behave as one wishes, liberated from the expected behaviour of a true Sabra [Israeli-born], healthy in body and soul. One can enjoy all the things which one missed without even knowing that one

missed them: order, self-restraint, lifestyle, urban culture and good manners.[15]

Furthermore, as Sh. Shifra has noted, 'Hebrew literature sought many escape routes just so that it should not have to face our own real image. A great deal of courage is required for this kind of confrontation, especially after the Holocaust.'[16] Escaping abroad is one way of reflecting this in the world of fiction. Europe is presented as a challenge, which puts the culture of the Sabra under scrutiny. It is easier to ask fundamental questions about the nature of the whole Israeli national enterprise when placing the fictional characters afar. From this vantage point it is also easier, as Rubinstein suggested, to 'rediscover the lost conceptual paradise of Tel Aviv'. A. B. Yehoshua, whose work is discussed in Chapter 2, commented about his own stay in Paris between 1963 and 1967: 'The distance seemed to help me accept Israeli reality.'[17] Distance in this case serves not so much the purpose of discovering the 'other', as of examining the self. True, Lacan reminds us that Freud's essential insight was that one bears otherness within oneself, and that 'man's desire finds its meaning in the desire of the other, not so much because the other holds the key to the object desired, as because the first object of desire is to be recognised by the other'.[18] The Israeli characters who go abroad are seeking something different: they seek not only to examine their 'self' but also to redefine their identity. Yaakov Shavit, in his discussion on the dialectical distinction between Jews and non-Jews, suggests that 'an encounter with a foreign culture which attains a close yet oppositional status leads to a conflict, which in turn initiates a complex, dialectical process of discovery and even of re-structuring the self'.[19] He claims the dialectical tension between 'inside' and 'outside' is an inseparable part of cultural history. The outside provides a vantage point which enables the onlooker to see a clearer picture of the whole 'inside' and to compare it with the 'outside'. Like Bakhtin, he believes that 'otherness' is a powerful factor in our understanding of our selves.[20]

Every period in history has its real and imaginary journeys. The protagonists of Romantic travel stories sought adventure, something alien and exotic, as well as solitude. The journey itself was often the aim, not necessarily its destination. At times it was seen as a journey into the mind, blurring the distinction between actual and ideal reality. Many leading twentieth-century authors also wrote about the 'big voyage', an escape from the deadly humdrum routine in which their protagonists were trapped, and their search for redemption. During the 1920s and 1930s the journey and life as a journey became dominant themes in English literature.[21] All these endless and often meaningless journeys are a warped reincarnation of the Odyssean epic. Nevertheless, they all involve promise, hope and renewal, despite the sorrows incurred. The Israeli poet Nathan Zach has pointed out that these Odyssean characteristics continued throughout the long history of Mediterranean culture and far beyond:

> The symbol of the journey and all that it involves – the sense of mission, of yearning for revelation, for renewal, for the improvement of the world and of the soul, for reacquaintance with all that had been and was now lost, or that which never was, everything brilliant which had tarnished or had been concealed in the wearying routine, the intoxicating charm of the big adventure with all its dangers, as well as the prospect of self-fulfilment - all these have long become archetypes in our private and collective consciousness and are repeated motifs and structures in the history of culture and literature.[22]

The Hebrew version of the 'big voyage' goes right back to God's command to Abram (as he was then called): 'Leave your own country, your kinsmen, and your father's house, and go to the country that I will show you.'[23] The Israeli anthropologists Zali Gurevich and Gideon Aran have suggested that whilst in many religions, and particularly in archaic religions, the place serves as the basis of identity, this is not the case in Judaism. They argue that God's command to Abram legitimised a state of constant movement, which explains Judaism's rejection of an absolute and harmonious identification with place.[24] They

7

distinguish between two different concepts of place. One is termed the 'small place' and is characterised by its concrete local markers, such as a house, a street, landscape or language. The other is termed the 'big place' and is associated with an idea, rather than with any specific place. When applying this thesis to Jewish history, the idea underlying the 'big place' is that of 'the Land', and by extension 'the Promised Land'. It is a place at which one arrives, leaves and returns to, but to which one can never belong.[25] This idea is by no means generally accepted, and is criticised for confining itself to the philosophical, theological and cultural aspects of the Jews' relationship with the Land, excluding altogether the political aspect of Jews and Arabs claiming the same territory. It has been pointed out that although the Promised Land was an inherent feature of Rabbinic Judaism, it was marginalised in order to help to unify the people of Israel and their Torah in their exilic existence.[26] Be this as it may, the issue of movement has become linked with issues of identity. Coincidentally, this is similar to the state of mind of modern humanity, which has lost its sense of belonging. Escaping from one single thought, one identity and one place, we find the idea of place has become empty and our modern consciousness has become a 'homeless mind', never quite finding its place. It has been suggested by Gurevich and Aran that Zionism was an attempt to link the two irreconcilable concepts of the 'little place' with the 'big place'.[27] However, A. B. Yehoshua contends that Zionism failed to tie Jewish consciousness to one place. He claims that the 'parasitic' aspect of Jewish identity is built into its structure, and this undesirable characteristic has enabled Jews for generations to wander from place to place amongst other nations, not returning to their own homeland. Like Gurevich and Aran, he can see the conflict between the Jewish need to wander and yet to belong to one place.[28]

The search for a 'locus' is also expressed in Israeli visual art. Sarit Shapira, in her exhibition catalogue *Routes of Wandering*, suggests that this search by artists should be seen not only as a sociological, historical and intellectual phenomenon, but also as part of a continuing search for the self.[29] It inevitably results in the need to move about, rather than being bound by a fixed place and a fixed identity. The dialectics between 'here' and 'there' in the second half of the twentieth century, which pre-occupied the later phase of the modernist period, are updated by Shapira to post-modernist discussions of the concepts of wandering, movement and questioning. She argues that the modernist hierarchial distinction between centre and periphery does not exist, because there is no fixed centre. Her proposed concept of wandering is modelled on the French post-modernist interpretation of movement, that it lacks centre, purpose or direction. Judaism too rejects one centre. In a critique of the exhibition organised by Shapira, M. Geldman pointed out that whilst wandering was not regarded by Judaism as negative, barren movement, nevertheless it was the first punishment ever given to man and woman in the Bible:

> This was the punishment given to Adam and Eve who were cast out of the Garden of Eden. It was also the punishment given to the first murderer, as well as to the Jews who sinned against their God who had chosen them as His people. On the other hand, wandering appears in the Bible as movement towards the right place, towards God who Himself is referred to [subsequently] as 'the Place'.[30]

Along the same lines, Dan Miron has argued that protagonists in Israeli cultural life are continually seeking some sort of a locus, a definite place in time and space, which might reveal authentic reality.[31] But, he points out, the 'locus' moves around several places so that it can suit the desired self-image of the characters. Consequently, the place is perceived subjectively. The idea of a constant search for the one place underlies Yitzhak Orpaz's idea of the 'secular pilgrim'.[32] He compares many characters in contemporary novels with pilgrims, except that being secular, they lack a holy place. Like pilgrims, they are in a state of unrest, in constant movement, which becomes a purpose in itself. The characters are inherently strangers wherever they are found, forever seeking the unattainable, and forever unable to settle down in any one place. In these stories, the psychological state of the pilgrims is more important than their physical surroundings.

Places can become either metaphors or metonyms for reality: Europe can be a place not only conceived of in its literal significance, but also given a literary function. René Wellek, on the question of the setting, noted that

> Romantic description aims at establishing and maintaining a mood: plot and characterization are to be dominated by tone, effect. . . . Naturalistic description is a seeming documentation, offered in the interest of illusion. Setting is environment; and environments, especially domestic interiors, may be viewed as metonymic, or metaphoric, expressions of character. . . . Setting may be the expression of a human will. It may, if it is a natural setting, be a projection of the will. . . . Again, setting may be the massive determinant – environment viewed as physical or social causation, something over which the individual has little individual control.[33]

This study of six novels demonstrates some of the poetic uses of place and explores further literary possibilities. The place can stand in the centre of the novel, with the protagonist just highlighting it, or the place can be presented in realist terms but so that it emphasises the meanings which the work seeks to communicate.[34] This is the case of Y. Amichai's *Not of This Time, Not of This Place* (Chapter 6). Sometimes the description of an actual place is compared or contrasted with another place, or their respective social and cultural aspects are contrasted. These are the treatments in A. B. Yehoshua's *Molcho* (Chapter 2) and Benjamin Tammuz's *Minotaur* (Chapter 4), two of the novels examined in this book.[35] In *Molcho* the place's function is to reinforce the characterisation of the protagonist: there is an analogy between the dull landscape and the protagonist. In *Minotaur* there is also an analogous comparison of places and what they represent culturally, but here the comparison serves to express the ideology of a pan-Mediterranean culture. In other works, place is used as a tool for analysis of the soul, for

10

externalising place images can reveal the inner places of the psyche, as exemplified in Yaakov Shabtai's *Past Perfect* (Chapter 1).[36] Place here is presented in the dialectical terms of home and abroad, and is used primarily as a poetic tool for the psychological analysis of the protagonist. Place can also be metonymic, endowed with virtues that have no objective foundation. Once this happens, detailed descriptions are reduced and become secondary in their importance. This can be seen in Ruth Almog's *Death in the Rain* where the descriptions of Israel are metaphorical but those of Greece are metonymic.[37] The relationship between the two places is brought about by juxtaposition, rather than by relying on essential resemblance to create the metonymy. Descriptions of place can serve to strengthen 'objective realism', yet when the description assumes additional layers and the place becomes a metaphor or metonym, 'subjective realism' is created, which blurs the objective place.[38] In Shlomo Nitzan's *The Private Empire of Zmiri-Picasso* (Chapter 5), descriptions of places in Israel and abroad are realistic, but a comparison between the two reveals that, in addition, the landscape in Israel has become metaphorical, blurring the perception of the objective place: the mountains and the sea are metaphors for Arab terrorism, and the open countryside with its memorials stands for war and death.[39] The sea also represents the concept of a pan-Mediterranean culture, which Tammuz and Almog address directly in their novels, and Yehoshua and Nitzan incorporate indirectly.

Situating the protagonists between home and abroad in their search to redefine Israeli identity, these writers came to a common conclusion: Israeli identity should derive its ideology from the concept of a Mediterranean culture shared by all the peoples of the region. Without the perspective of time, it would be too bold to suggest that this thesis is the most significant in Israeli writing today, but it certainly should be taken seriously. The emergence of two journals devoted to Mediterranean studies is corroboration of its great interest also outside fiction.[40] Whilst there are obviously doubts that there can be one comprehensive unit comprising the many different nations and religions in the region, the consensus emerging from the journals is

11

that nevertheless the idea of a Mediterranean culture does exist. It would include pluralism and the construction of an ideal modelled on Hellenistic culture, which tolerated co-existence and interaction of different peoples, landscapes, histories, tongues and cultures. This ideal is attractive in the search for Israeli identity.

That search has preoccupied the Jewish people in Israel and in the Diaspora for more than two hundred years. It most probably began with the arrival of secularism at the end of the eighteenth century, when the Jewish Enlightenment rejected religion as the only determining component of Jewish identity, and nationalism in the form of Zionism was offered as an alternative. However, while Zionism was being fulfilled in the twentieth century, new secular options were explored, including the short-lived Canaanite movement (1944–53), which believed in a historical link and political co-operation between the Hebrews and the Phoenicians. (The Phoenician civilisation spread throughout the Mediterranean and is thought to be the ancestor of Greek culture.) The Canaanite movement claimed that there had been a cultural and religious partnership between Israel and its neighbours. Yaakov Shavit explains that 'the aim of [the Canaanite movement], which sought to lessen Israel's historical isolation and to consider Israel as an integral part of its environment and culture, was not to lower its key historical value. The goal was to place it at the focal point of a very broad cultural milieu.'[41] He goes on to point out that Canaanism was not an isolated ideology, but similar in its basic premises and structures to others found in various Mediterranean countries. One of the reasons for its failure in Israel must have been its disregard of the history of the Jews' exilic existence, and its countering of the view of the religious uniqueness of the Jewish people. To be an Israeli is to have physical links with the land of Israel and with its language, not necessarily with Jewish culture, tradition and religion.[42] Canaanism was a manifestation of the crisis in secular national Judaism, the same crisis which led five years later to the Mediterranean ideology. Time will tell if this option will find a wider response.

Only after selecting the texts for analysis did I realise that, other than Amichai's novel, they were all published in the 1980s, yet this is not, of course, coincidental. The concept of a period, whether in history at large or in literary history, is an interpretation, a selection and grouping of facts, collectively generated and modified by an endless process of redescription. The 1980s were probably the most prolific period in the development of the literature of the State of Israel, of prose in particular. The Lebanon War at the beginning of the decade, and the war of the Intifada at the end, aroused heated political controversies which in turn were reflected in contemporary literature. The writings of the 1980s are highly political, reacting directly to the political, ideological and social reality. Whereas this was unacceptable to the poetic consensus of the 1960s, the involvement of the authors and their works in the political arena during the 1970s, and more so during the 1980s, was embraced and made aesthetically legitimate. Both the critics and the reading public accepted and expected this mode of writing. This is certainly true for Shabtai, Yehoshua, Almog, Tammuz and Nitzan. They started their literary careers in the 1960s, but their later works reflect this change to political engagement. Yitzhak Oren has noticed that the change is particularly discernible in the characterisation of the protagonists.[43] They are no longer passive, defeated anti-heroes but rather protagonists who are prepared to confront difficulties and who strive to improve their condition. They are Israelis who struggle with specific Israeli problems rather than anonymous characters who struggle with universal existential problems. It has been suggested that neo-romanticism and post-modernism are the most suitable styles for exploring such problems.[44] It is certainly true that in the optimistic spirit of neo-romanticism, the authors studied in this book have shattered old myths in order to create new ones. Plots have also changed, and family and genealogical sagas are dominant. Oren suggests that the broader novel rather than the short story is best suited for these plots, hence its extensive use. The main themes in many of these novels are Zionist and Sabra ideologies. Questioning and examining the two lead to another theme, of particular interest to us, and that is the search for the self, particularly *vis-à-vis* Jewish identity.

The chapters that follow analyse the search for the self when the protagonists are placed between home and abroad, between here and there, between Israel and Europe.

NOTES

For the purposes of this research, I have not followed one particular scheme of transliteration, but chose to follow Israeli spoken pronunciation.

1. Yehuda Amichai, *Me'ahorei kol zeh mistater osher gadol (Behind All This Hides Great Happiness)* (Jerusalem and Tel Aviv: Schocken, 1974), p.22.
2. S. Y. Agnon, 'Ido ve-Inam' ('Ido and Inam'), *Ad Henah (Unto Here)* (Tel Aviv: Schocken, 1971), p.352.
3. Gaston Bachelard, *The Poetics of Space* (Boston: Beacon Press, 1969), pp.211–16.
4. Robert Alter, 'Afterword: A Problem of Horizons', in E. Anderson (ed.), *Contemporary Israeli Literature* (Philadelphia: Jewish Publication Society of America, 1977), pp.326–38.
5. Ibid., p.336.
6. Alan Mintz, *'Banished from Their Father's Table': Loss of Faith and Hebrew Autobiography* (Bloomington: Indiana University Press, 1989), p.96. Professor Shmuel Werses, in his illuminating paper 'The Houses of Berdichevsky', published in *Mehkarei Yerushalayim basifrut (Jerusalem Studies in Hebrew)*, No. 5 (1984), pp.63–94, pointed out that this tension can already be found in early writers such as Mendele, H. N. Bialik and M. Y. Berdichevsky. In the case of Berdichevsky, the dichotomy is indeed between the secluded Jewish village and that which is 'beyond the river', the alluring wide horizon of the enlightened non-Jewish world outside the village.
7. David Lodge, *Working with Structuralism* (London: Routledge & Kegan Paul, 1981), p.9.
8. Mary Lynn Broe and Angela Ingram (eds), *Women's Writing in Exile,* (Chapel Hill and London: University of North Carolina, 1989), p.4.
9. Cited by Susan Stanford Friedman, 'Exile in the American Grain', in ibid., p.101.
10. Cited by Tony Tanner, 'Additions to the World', *The Times Literary Supplement*, 14 Aug. 1992.
11. See John Taylor, 'Painless Progress', *The Times Literary Supplement*, 25 Sept. 1992, pp.13–14.
12. Many of the Second Aliya (Second Wave of Immigration) writers, such as Y. H. Brenner, A. Reuveni, Y. Zarhi and Agnon, portrayed expatriates.
13. See Yaffa Berlovitz, *E'ebra na ba'aretz (Wandering in the Land)* (Tel Aviv: Misrad Habitahon, 1992), pp.343–71.
14. Gershon Shaked, 'Besof ma'arav' ('At the End of the West'), *Hadoar* (31

Oct. 1986), LXV: 40 (2831), p.16.

15. Amnon Rubinstein, *Liheyot am hofshi (To Be a Free People)* (Jerusalem and Tel Aviv: Schocken, 1977), p.112.

16. Sh. Shifra, 'Zara bimkomah' ('Stranger in her own Place'), *Yediot Aharonot*, 27 Nov. 1987.

17. Cited by Joseph Cohen, *Voices of Israel* (State University of New York Press, 1990), p.47.

18. Cited by Malcolm Bowie, *Freud, Proust and Lacan: Theory as Fiction* (Cambridge University Press, 1988), p.201.

19. Yaakov Shavit, *Hayahadut bir'ee hayavnut (Judaism in the Greek Mirror and the Emergence of the Modern Hellenized Jew)* (Tel Aviv: Am Oved, 1992), p.24.

20. Ibid., p.35.

21. Paul Fussell, *Abroad: British Literary Traveling Between the Wars* (New York: Oxford University Press, 1980), pp.52–5.

22. Nathan Zach, 'Hamasa hagadol' ('The Big Voyage'), *Igra, Almanac for Literature and Art* (Jerusalem: Carmel, 1990), pp.149–200.

23. Genesis 12: 1 (New English Bible).

24. Zali Gurevich and Gideon Aran, 'Al hamakom (Antropologia Yisra'elit)' ('About the Place [Israeli Anthropology]'), *Alpayim* 4 (1991), pp.9–44.

25. This thesis has been severely criticised by Yitzhak Laor, who claimed that the introspective attitude deliberately overlooks other problems which are associated with the place, such as the existence of the Arabs and the Israelis' relationships with them. Anthropologists such as Gurevich and Aran read the place as an ideologically cohesive text, but one written collectively by the establishment, in which the Arabs have no part. Laor accused them of excluding these problems when discussing the place, even though such problems might not be directly linked with issues of identity. See 'Kotvim et ha'aretz' ('Writing the Country'), *Ha'aretz*, 31 Jan. 1992.

26. See Baruch Kimmerling, 'Al da'at hamakom' ('On the use of the term "place" as a surrogate for deity'), *Alpayim* 6 (1992), pp.57–68. He argues that Gurevich and Aran's thesis is unsubstantiated, and that Judaism does not have an ambivalent attitude to place.

27. This was also the case with artists of the turn of the century, who painted Biblical landscapes and people, which belong to the 'big place', through the concrete landscape and images of the Arabs, which belong to the 'small place'. More recent painters came to the conclusion that there was no possible bridge between the two places. On this interesting parallel between art and literature, see Itamar Levy, 'Hayehudi hamudhak' ('The Suppressed Jew'), *Ha-Aretz*, 13 March 1992.

28. 'Avraham B. Yehoshua', *Ma'ariv*, 28 June 1991.

29. Sarit Shapira, *Maslulei nedudim (Routes of Wandering)*, exh. cat., The Israel Museum (Jerusalem, 1991). See also Itamar Levy, 'Le'an nodedim hanedudim' ('Where do wanderings wander?'), *Ha-Aretz*, 6 March 1992.

15

30. M. Geldman, 'Maslulei nedudim' (Routes of Wandering), *Ah'shav* 58 (Spring/Summer 1992), p.245. Note also Geldman's contention that whilst there is no doubt as to the centrality of the subject of wandering for the Israeli, either because of its archetypal status in Jewish history, or because of the collapse of the Zionist ethos, Shapira ignores the contribution of the media in creating a new 'place'. Through the media, the 'place' has shifted from God, from its holy or secular geography, to the small, isolated 'locale', where real existence now takes place. Geldman expresses it in his poem about Andy Warhol: 'I am photographed, therefore I exist.'

31. Dan Miron, *Im lo tiheye Yerushalayim (If There is no Jerusalem)* (Tel Aviv: Hakibbutz Hameuchad, 1987), pp.227–8.

32. Yitzhak Orpaz, *Hatzalian hahiloni (The Secular Pilgrim)* (Tel Aviv: Hakibbutz Hameuchad, 1982).

33. René Wellek and Austin Warren, *Theory of Literature* (Harmondsworth: Penguin Books, 1973), p.221.

34. See Nurit Govrin, 'Yerushalayim ve-Tel Aviv kemetaphorot basifrut ha'ivrit: hitpathuta shel tadmit' ('Jerusalem and Tel Aviv as Metaphors in Hebrew Literature: Development of an Image'), *Yerushalayim batoda'ah uva'asiyah hatzionit (Jerusalem in Zionist Consciousness and Action)* (Jerusalem: Hebrew University, 1989), pp.434–50.

35. A. B. Yehoshua, *Molcho* (Tel Aviv: Hakibbutz Hameuchad, 1987); Benjamin Tammuz, *Minotaur* (Tel Aviv: Hakibbutz Hameuchad, 1980).

36. Yaakov Shabtai, *Sof davar* (Tel Aviv: Siman Kriah/Hakibbutz Hameuchad, 1984), trans Dalya Bilu, *Past Perfect* (New York: Viking Penguin, 1987).

37. Ruth Almog, *Mavet Bageshem (Death in the Rain)* (Jerusalem: Keter Publishing House, 1982).

38. See also Menucha Gilboa, 'America kemakom, kemetaphora ukesemel bishlosha romanim' ('America as a place, a metaphor and a symbol in three novels'), in Stanley Nash (ed.), *Migvan* (Lod: Habberman Institute for Research in Literature, 1988), p.115.

39. Shlomo Nitzan, *Ha'imperia hapratit shel Zmiri-Picasso (The Private Empire of Zmiri-Picasso)* (Tel Aviv: Sifriyat Hapoalim, 1982).

40. *Mediterranean Language Review* (Wiesbaden: Harrassowitz Verlag), and *Mediterranean Historical Review* (London: Frank Cass).

41. Yaakov Shavit, *The New Hebrew Nation: A Study in Heresy and Fantasy*, (London: Frank Cass, 1987), p.92. See also pp.90–1 below (pp.15–16 of *Minotaur*).

42. See also B. Kurtzweil, *Sifrutenu hahadasha: hemshech o mahapecha (Our New Literature: Continuation or Revolution)* (Jerusalem and Tel Aviv: Schocken, 1959), pp.270–300.

43. Yitzhak Oren, *Hatzda'ah lasifrut ha-Yisra'elit (Salute to Israeli Literature)* (Rishon Letzion: Yahad, 1991), pp.32–9.

44. See Ortsion Bartana, *Shmonim (The Eighties)* (Tel Aviv: Agudat Hasofrim, 1993), pp.19–47.

1

Past Perfect

by YAAKOV SHABTAI

Past Perfect is the second and last novel by Yaakov Shabtai, published after his untimely death at the age of 47 in August 1981. It is relevant to know this about the author because the illness and fear of death that dominated Shabtai's own life are also present in his fictional world. Indeed, Shabtai had not completed his novel before he died after a long illness. It was left for his widow, Edna, with Professor Dan Miron, to edit and prepare the unfinished 1,200 manuscript pages for publication. In the Afterword they describe the daunting task of having to choose and decide on the definitive version of the book, which was particularly difficult because Shabtai used to rewrite obsessively nearly every sentence. As Edna Shabtai testified:

> With compulsive tendency to examine [it] anew, again and again, changing the order of the words, their melody, their rhythm, with great seriousness and a terrifying sense of artistic responsibility. He would sit and fill entire pages with synonyms, near-synonyms, nascent and renascent sentences sprouting out of one another with an infinite wealth of variation and alternatives which he would later cut down and concentrate, as if they were crystals.[1]

This process is further echoed in Edna Shabtai's fictional autobiography:

> The first chapter was in front of her, a huge pile consisting of more than six hundred pages. She was daunted by the number of repetitions of the same sentence, the same idea, the same action, written in four, five and even seven variations. Endless versions and parts of versions all intertwined with one another accompanied by editorial comments and suggestions.[2]

17

However, as Miron has quite rightly pointed out, this extra-literary information should not bias our evaluation of the novel and 'the text itself should absorb our full attention' (p.243).

The novel is comprised of four rather unevenly finished chapters, which is hardly surprising given its unusual genesis. The first chapter was edited by Edna Shabtai and Dan Miron, the second was the only one to be finished by the author himself, the third chapter was nearly completed by him, and the last was once again completed by the two editors.

The powerful and long opening sentence of the novel encapsulates much of that which follows: the downhill slope towards the death of Meir, the protagonist, a 42-year-old engineer, married with two sons. Distance (space) and time work in unison to bring this process to its inevitable conclusion – the end of his life or 'the end of the matter', as the Hebrew title, *Sof davar*, can be translated. Thus, space and time are clearly of paramount importance. In the past, both were thought of as a fixed arena in which events took place, unaffected by those events. Today, in the general theory of relativity they are considered to be dynamic qualities[3] and this is how they are conceived in *Past Perfect*.

The Hebrew title alludes to the penultimate verse in the last chapter of the book of Ecclesiastes : 'Let us hear the conclusion of the whole matter: Fear God, and keep his commandments: for this is the whole duty of man.'[4] This 'conclusion' is juxtaposed with the well-known dictum declared earlier in the same chapter, and which sets the tone of Ecclesiastes: 'Vanity of vanities, saith the preacher; all is vanity.' Another verse in this chapter is also relevant to Shabtai and the writing of *Past Perfect*: 'And further, by these, my son, be admonished; of making many books there is no end, and much study is weariness of the flesh.' Yet despite this advice Shabtai did set about writing his book, an ironic, sceptical response to the Ecclesiastical 'conclusion'. To introduce irony into the story itself, Shabtai employs third-person narration that is objective and detached at times, but which subjectively presents value judgements at others. In a subtle way the narration might shift altogether – even if in mid-sentence – and become a stream-of-consciousness

18

narrative. The shift creates a gap between the reader and the narrator, allowing irony and very often humour as well.

When we first meet the protagonist he is already a sick man and is seized by a fear of illness and of death itself. Because of the subjective narration, there is no indication as to how to evaluate the extent of his condition. The excessive descriptions of the illness, which dominate all Meir's movements, moods and thoughts, raise the suspicion that he might be exaggerating. Only in the third chapter does it become absolutely clear that he is in fact a dying man and this late realisation is shocking and disturbing to the reader. Meir's jealousy, which always 'accompanied his life like a shadow' (p. 20), now assumes ridiculous dimensions. This, coupled with his quick and extreme changes of mood, indicates his psychological state of mind, which is bound up with his continuous preoccupation with his physical condition. He is jealous of healthy-looking people and finds comfort neither in Dr Reiner's reassuring words nor in those of his friend Posner when he says 'there is no such thing as an ideal state of health any more than there is such thing as an ideal state altogether. Health is actually a state which one desires and from which one continually and inevitably becomes distanced' (p.29; see also p.28).[5] When Meir observes his body he expresses his horror: 'the vitality of the suppleness and strength are lost for ever, and this diseased flesh will dry up, become weak and will increasingly lose its shape' (p.33). He feels that his body betrays him (pp.65–6) and comes to realise that there is no escape from death. Throughout his illness Meir feels 'as if imprisoned inside a bubble which is closing around him and which separates him from the world' (p.190). Shabtai uses the metaphor of a divide, or a partition, with increased intensity as the story progresses, corresponding with the protagonist's gradual separation from life.

The whole book is extraordinarily authentically narrated from the point of view of an insider, allowing the reader to share an experience which is rarely presented in Hebrew prose. Its impact is particularly powerful when one knows about Shabtai's own experience of illness and the fear of death. In her fictional autobiography, his widow observes:

19

With increasing amazement she saw how David took his body and soul, as well as other tools from his life which he knew intimately, and despite the cliches he created a prism through which he could reflect what was for him the essence, the very essence of life – which is the process of the inevitable separation of man from the world; and he did it in the way which he himself especially knew and experienced. (p.69)

The sense of separation is developed in *Past Perfect* through the recurring imagery of wrapping or enveloping.[6] Very often the protagonist feels as if he is wrapped by silence, by darkness or by his moods. At times objects appear to him as if they too were veiled and remote. He is losing his direct touch with reality and starts to search for an alternative existence. His constant attraction to the sky suggests a means to one such alternative: he wants to be liberated and to be able to fly away. At its extreme, this wish leads him to escape to a hallucinatory world, as in this passage:

he raised himself to the heights of the sky and from there gazed towards the darkness, which was the Past side of the small blot of light stretched below him. People were standing there in its bright circle, their lit faces were familiar to him. . . . Then he looked towards the even greater darkness, at the Future side of the small blot, and he saw within the boundary of the ever-clouding light, shapeless features, though not entirely unrecognisable. (p.117)

Hallucinating in Freudian theory is a regression, or return to infantile ways, and this is just what happens to Meir. Unconsciously he craves the enveloping comfort of the womb and of childhood, and ultimately he finds his metaphysical redemption through his re-birth. Nearly all of the final chapter describes his hallucinations about the unknown domain that lies between life and death, and during these last moments he feels as if he were lying in a cradle. As Meir's illness progresses, his emotional and physical condition worsens: he shows various symptoms, including the disturbing but crucial hallucination of

20

a split personality: 'He felt as if he had a double, who one day in the future would be born. He actually felt him in his body, as if it was his double who filled him like the stuffing which fills a pillow' (p.143).

It is ironic that it is in London, the very place Meir goes to find rest from his pains, that the illness overpowers him. In one of the most astonishing and moving passages in the book, Shabtai describes what it feels like to collapse with sickness, going into the most minute sensations of Meir's panic, fear and pain:

> He bent down to the lower shelf and started to browse through the books which were there, his face perspiring and his glasses misting. He took out a book – this was not the book which Posner wanted – and he got up to wipe his face and his glasses, and whilst doing so he felt as if the floor underneath his feet was moving and slanting. He leant against the bookcase and looked anxiously around him, hoping that it would pass, but the movement, which seemed for a moment a little less did not stop; as well as this, he felt the lightness in his limbs disappearing and they became thick and heavy, and as he observed the movement of the floor and the draining sensation of his limbs, he walked very slowly, dragging his feet – he was incapable of doing more than that – towards the salesman. All of a sudden, everything both around him and inside him became distant, and moved with a dreadful slowness and dullness. He told the salesman that he was feeling unwell and asked if he could have some water. He felt his face become petrified, as if it was fixed inside a dry, stretched outer skin, in which was a pair of eyes with a frozen look. His voice broke through his lips with a terrible slowness, and sounded hollow to him, as if it was rising from clay pipes in the depths of the earth. (p.187)

The fear of this physical deterioration drives Meir to an obsessive fear of impotence which contributes to his sexual

21

fixation. He himself realises that this fixation is also linked to his psychological make-up: 'He felt that all this was a result of a weakness in character and of lack of confidence' (p.195). Indeed, his disappointment with his inability to fulfil his wild sexual dreams has affected his thoughts and behaviour ever since his unconsummated sexual experience as a young man with his friend's wife. Despite the belief in free love, in which he and his friends were brought up, he finds it difficult to realise that in fact he prefers a conventional domestic existence. Another event, unrelated to his illness, which contributes to his sexual obsession, is the discovery that unexpectedly his wife has succeeded where he failed: she did have the courage to have a brief affair outside marriage and away from domesticity. His jealousy, coupled with his childish naivety, is pathetic. The reader is also aware of the humorous aspect of his embarrassment even with looking at sex books, which he nervously regards as a perversity. His sexual attraction to every female he sees, particularly to young girls of lower social and intellectual levels than his own (such as an office girl, a bank clerk, a waitress, a hotel receptionist, or a casual teenage tourist) all comes to nothing. The only time he actually lets go is with his doctor and that, a final irony, ends with his death. One of the reasons for going abroad is to let loose his fantasies with prostitutes; however, the reader knows by that stage that this wish, like his others, will not be fulfilled. Once when he goes so far as actually to invite a girl to the cinema – where he often seeks refuge from his sufferings – he is greatly relieved to discover when they go back to her hotel after the film that her room is occupied and his courtship can end before it has even started. His sense of disappointment follows him to Amsterdam. From the moment he arrives there he plans to go to the Red Light district, yet despite his constant attempts to find it, the nearest he gets is to locate it on the map – along with itineraries which he plans all the time but which also come to nothing.

Apart from the protagonist, there are only a few characters in the story, all of whom are presented mainly from Meir's viewpoint: his wife, his parents and his two close friends. His friend Gavrosh has died before the story opens, and his parents

22

die during the course of the story. It is thus his friend Posner who knows him the longest and who plays an important part in his life. Meir's two friends represent two opposing approaches to death with Meir oscillating between them. As Oren has pointed out, Posner represents the secular and rational hedonistic approach that believes only in the pleasures of the moment, since there is nothing after death.[7] Gavrosh, on the other hand, represents a religious mystical approach that believes in life after death. Posner stands for everything that Meir would like to be but which he is not. Posner is tanned, healthy (though he smokes) and practises the ideological and social doctrines in which they both believed in their youth. He has left his wife and lives with a much younger student of his in an unconventional lifestyle. We are never sure that this is purely by his own choice, but Meir admires him and feels inferior to him. Unlike Meir, Posner is a fatalist whose scepticism balances Meir's counter-arguments, without which Meir could not exist. However, Posner's political and moral beliefs are not clear, and Shabtai himself testified that he had problems moulding this character (p.245).

The same can be said about Gavrosh, who clearly has had a great influence on Meir's life, yet the main information we have about him is his passion for nature, which emphasises and stands in complete contrast to Meir's passion for urban surroundings. Once again, the friend is not fully developed: he seems to be there to mould the protagonist. Meir's wife also fulfils the same function of establishing the protagonist's character, rather than emerging in her own right. Their sons too hardly feature.

The characterisation of Meir's father presents a real flaw. Shabtai was aware of the problem and commented in his notes: 'the father is important!!! check it!!! enrich!!!' (p.245). The father represents the pioneer who in his youth must have had the courage to act upon his socialist beliefs. Subsequently the problems of everyday life, which weigh heavily on him, dull his spirits and drain him emotionally and intellectually. Meir despises him for this. Even after his mother's death he cannot sympathise with his father's loneliness and despair.

23

It seems to me that only in the characterisation of the mother is Shabtai successful. She grows into a full person in some of the most beautiful passages in the novel. In complete contrast with the father, she does not succumb to the boredom of her narrow existence, but continues to live a much richer life, albeit in her dreams and her imagination. She is self-effacing, good-hearted and happy to please everyone around her. Meir is annoyed with his mother's attitude to herself yet he enjoys her efforts to spoil him, particularly with delicious food, which he feels he should not accept because he is on a diet:

> And after serious consideration, struggling with herself, she said carefully as if risking her life, that she knew she should not offer him any food, she would offer him some beef with a small side dish of peppers. She said this as if walking a tightrope whilst seized by feelings of guilt and apology. Since Meir accepted his defeat and did not immediately express firm resistance, she continued saying that it was a very lean meat, without any fat, and Meir, who was still struggling as if undefeated, smiled vaguely and said, but without resolution, that this was against the doctor's instructions, that it would ruin his diet, and his mother said that once only could not ruin anything. She suggested that he accompany her, if he wished, to the kitchen to see with his own eyes how lean the meat was so that he could then decide for himself. Meir got up and accompanied her to the kitchen and said that he had not yet decided whether to become a vegetarian for the rest of his life but that nevertheless he wished to give it a try, in case it improved his health, and then his mother took out of the fridge the bowl of meat, put it near him so that he could see for himself how lean it was and enquired if perhaps he would prefer a piece of fish which was also very lean, and Meir said repeatedly 'you ruin my diet', and without even indicating his consent he sat down at his usual place. (pp.75–6)

The obvious question is why Shabtai came to neglect these characters. Miron explains by reminding us that Shabtai suggested that this story should be seen as a continuation of his first novel, *Past Continuous* (p.245). The difficulty must have been in isolating the protagonist from his social context and in focusing only on him. The social context, fully represented in the first novel, disappears here, enabling the existential aspect of its disintegration to be considered. The representation of this kind of existentialism is criticised by Bartana. He accuses the majority of contemporary Israeli writers, Shabtai included, of being unable to detatch themselves from contemporary events relating to everyday existence, and of not elevating this reality to the more philosophical issues of 'Existentialism'.[8] However, it seems to me that this is just what Shabtai manages to achieve in *Past Perfect*.

Place

I would now like to examine one specific element in the narrative structure – 'place'. As in Shabtai's first novel, place, and particularly Tel Aviv, plays a most important role on both the thematic and the structural levels of the text. The first chapter is set in Tel Aviv, the second is still anchored in Tel Aviv (though Meir prepares for his departure), the third is set abroad and the last is back in Israel. The repetitive and excessive descriptions of the various locations point to the place's importance in the dynamics of the text and suggest more than what is actually described. An objectively described place becomes less important than its poetic attributes and it assumes imaginative or figurative value. The story takes place in two locations – home and abroad. Home is confined to the city of Tel Aviv alone and abroad is also confined, to two cities. (Such exclusively urban descriptions in modern Hebrew literature deserve further study.) There are accurate details of the routes which Meir takes within the small section of the old part of Tel Aviv where he lives. Anywhere beyond this familiar and intimate area makes him feel uncomfortable (for example, pp.56, 60–1). He walks endlessly along the same old streets in his search for peace of mind, thinking that 'there is something comforting in these familiar streets' (p.14). Most of the time, though, he reflects dispassionately on the details of his surroundings, like the lense of a camera:

> and as he was walking along northwards, looking almost unconsciously at the pavement, the trees, the shops and the houses, he absorbed all their details with an unintentional glance, even most minute and nearly hidden ones. At the same time he absorbed all the changes which had occurred and considered what it must have been before the changes took place, like three photographs one on top of the other. (p.32)

Or on another occasion: 'as he was walking in the desolate street, he unconsciously absorbed the sight of the old houses with their dark courtyards and the pulled down fences. Here and there he saw a bush or a tree which looked like a column of darkness' (p.67).

This apparently unfocused yet detailed description of place corresponds, in my mind, to the concept of the unity of time and space, so important in this story. As mentioned earlier (p.18, this volume), that unity is introduced in the opening sentence of the novel. It is as if Shabtai were following Einstein's theory of relativity which postulates that 'every object must have not only length, width and height, but also duration in time. As a result, a complete description and location of an object must be given in terms of four co-ordinates.'[9] Full descriptions of location in the novel are reinforced by the pedantic naming of each and every street. This is done in an automatic, mechanical manner almost as in tourist guide books. Whilst the reader may become bored with these repetitions, Meir derives comfort from them and their familiarity is manifested by dropping the word 'street' after the name: 'he left the house and turned and went along Bograshov' (p.12) or 'and he crossed Dizengoff and turned into Emile Zola' (p.14).

There are surprisingly few descriptions of Tel Aviv itself other than of its streets, which always appear to be dark, desolate and cold. There is only an occasional reference to a busy square or to a few trees here and there.[10] A bookshop, a bakery, two restaurants, two coffee houses and two cinemas are mentioned, and the general impression on Meir is of a place devoid of life and excitement. As time progresses and as he reaches the divide which separates him from the world around him, the descriptions of the streets are more directly linked with his emotional moods:

> He crossed Brenner and Sheinkin as well as the market, surveying them with a glance, and was as empty and desolate as they were. And he walked on along Allenby and the end of King George, a street along which his mother must have passed hundreds or possibly thousands of times, and which somehow was identified with her life more than any other street and not just because she had passed there so many times. This street and a few of the surrounding streets were, for him, as if extensions of himself. (p.116; see also pp.117, 121)

One would expect that the constant mention of real street names in one small corner of Tel Aviv might help the reader to construct an illusion of the place. This process of recreation has been analysed by Wolfgang Iser:

> As we read, we oscillate to a greater or lesser degree between the building and the breaking of illusions. In a process of trial and error, we organize and reorganize the various data offered us by the text. These are the given factors, the fixed points on which we base our 'interpretation', trying to fit them together in the way we think the author meant them to be fitted. . . . The act of recreation is not a smooth or continuous process, but one which, in its essence, relies on interruptions of the flow to render it efficacious. We look forward, we look back, we decide, we change our decisions, we form expectations, we are shocked by their nonfulfillment, we question, we muse, we accept, we reject; this is the dynamic process of recreation.[11]

27

The mechanical, informative and detailed descriptions of Tel Aviv in *Past Perfect* raise the reader's expectations that, through the process of recreation, s/he will be able to conjure up an authentic image of the place. Yet these expectations are not fulfilled. It becomes apparent that it is not the place which is being actualised but the protagonist's inner world which is being revealed by the subjective presentation of the place.

Tel Aviv is also the setting for 11 of the 13 stories in Shabtai's *Hadod Peretz Mamri* (*Uncle Peretz Takes Off*, written between 1971 and 1981). As Edna Shabtai has pointed out, the city of those stories is a city of open spaces, of vineyards and of a wild undeveloped coastline.[12] In *Past Continuous* Shabtai changed the descriptions of his childhood city to portray it as ugly, densely populated and forgetful of its romantic past. His love for the city had given way to a sober antagonism to the Tel Aviv of his adulthood. In *Past Perfect*, Shabtai makes peace with the city. His attitude to Tel Aviv has undergone a full metamorphosis, from thesis to antithesis and on to synthesis.

It is the actual location which stands in the centre of this study rather than imaginary places or places remembered. However, *Past Perfect* provides us with the opportunity of comparing the descriptions of Tel Aviv when Meir is there with his descriptions from memory when he is abroad. When he is at home, he perceives Tel Aviv as a cold and desolate place. When thinking about it from afar, he remembers it as sunny, full of light and with blue skies extending well beyond the horizon of the city:

> . . . a pale sun appeared below the clouds and cast a cool patch of light on the street, and he thought longingly of Tel Aviv, with its yellowish white houses built as if of old cardboard, with its beaming blue skies, and in the centre, a little to the south, a sun as yellow as a yolk, as if painted by a child. And the skies stretched like a huge curtain over the sandy houses and over the hills and the citrus groves and the eucalyptus woods and the green sown fields. (p.171; see also pp.151, 166, 173)

Not only is the Tel Aviv of his memory sunny and bright, but its streets are filled with people – a fact to which he refers only once whilst at home (p.175).

There seems to be no tension between home and abroad in this text. The two places are juxtaposed to reveal the crucial role of place in the protagonist's life, and the threat of losing it: 'a feeling had seized him that Tel Aviv and its summer were nothing but a memory of something which had disappeared and dissolved and that he was an eternal exile' (p.175). In *Past Perfect*, the loss of a place in one's memory is as frightening as actually losing it. Meir's mother, representing the older generation born abroad, also experiences a similar sense of loss: 'when she reached the very place, her memory disintegrated and everything became blurred . . . a doubt arose in her that all this, after all, was nothing but an illusion' (p.48). Thus, the loss of a place, whether in actuality or in memory, can bring the daunting prospect of either an illusionary or an exilic existence. The possibility of this loss and what it would mean occur to both Meir and his mother in two opposite yet parallel situations: he reflects about home whilst being abroad and she reflects about abroad whilst being at home (there is a twist here in that abroad to Meir's mother was also her old home, and vice versa). Meir is afraid of losing the memory of home, which would result in him becoming an exile, whilst she is afraid of losing the memory of abroad and of becoming an exile in her own home. Both are in what the writer-in-exile Joseph Brodsky has defined as a 'condition we call exile'.[13] In a century of 'displacement' and 'misplacement', exile extends beyond geographical definition. Exile for Meir and his mother is a permanent diaspora, a state of alienation and a refusal to move to the centre, to be perpetually on the margin, at the fringes of the mainstream. Orpaz, besides defining this type of character as a 'secular pilgrim' (see p.9, this volume), has noted that many of them, just like Meir and his mother, discover that they are strangers and exiles within their own homes.[14]

Both Meir and his mother seek freedom abroad. They represent the two generations of Israel who, for different reasons, come back with the same realisation that there is no other place for them except home. Whilst Meir never doubts this conclusion, his mother, who is disillusioned with Israel, genuinely hopes to find a temporary substitute elsewhere. Yet, unlike Bill, her American friend who thrives on life as an eternal exile, she is tied to her country by her Zionist ideology, almost against her will:

> She suddenly found herself an exile in her own country, and she wanted to run away to the other end of the world, but almost against her wish she was tied to it not only by youth and childhood yearnings, by agitated hopes and memories, but also by the ties of heartaches and bitter resentment of her unfulfilled dreams and hopes. In the course of the years all of this had become a burden, yet the very essence of her life. (p.49)

Meir's mother is drawn by what lies beyond the here and now, by another existence. She wants to change one reality for another; her son seeks only a rest; but in the end a change of place does not bring meaningful change to either of them. Here Shabtai echoes Brenner's conclusion that place does not change the fortune of men and women. For Brenner, as for Meir's mother, leaving an exilic existence in favour of national redemption is a false hope. Belief in Zionism is therefore choice yet the noblest choice of all. Meir's unsuccessful and endless quest for freedom in the streets of Tel Aviv is only temporarily relieved by his attraction to the horizon and to the wide expanse of the sky above and beyond. Unlike his friend Gavrosh, he cannot find relief in the countryside and his frequent glances upwards express desperate attempts somehow to free himself and to fly away.

The theme of exit and return is often used in fiction, but in modern Hebrew literature it was particularly used by Brenner's generation of uprooted Hebrew writers, whose protagonists wander in vain from one place to another, nowhere finding peace of mind. As Gershon Shaked noted, for them 'the exit was not a stage in their development, but a total breakdown which at times brought about the ruin of the protagonist'.[15] In many respects I consider Shabtai's characters to be true descendants of Brenner's. His great influence on Shabtai is corroborated by Shabtai's notes in his 'general comments to chapter one' in *Past Perfect*: 'On the matter of description (and definition) of death in the beginning – glance at *Nerves* by Brenner' (p.245). Brenner's characters are doomed to failure as their exits (often initiated by unfulfilled erotic desires) lead them to a 'dead end'. They remain aliens in their new surroundings and – be it at home or abroad – the change of place does not help them change their destiny. Their struggles oscillate between accepting their fate and fighting it. These two polarised states of mind are represented by the mother and father, and the son in *Breakdown and Bereavement* and the echos reverberate in their contemporary counterparts in *Past Perfect*.

Meir cannot accept his fate and leaves for Amsterdam. The reader's expectations of a change in his condition in this new location correspond to his own expectations. In addition, the Israeli reader brings to the text the positive associations of this place, whose people courageously helped the Jews during the terrible period of persecution by Nazi Germany. Indeed, initial impressions of Amsterdam are favourable. For the first time in the story Meir notices and describes non-urban sights which he sees on his way from the airport, such as fields, small boats and even a tractor. However, soon enough he feels 'as if he was wrapped with the feeling of foreignness which could not be broken through' (p.128), and the feeling of being a stranger takes over and dominates his ceaseless wanderings of the streets of Amsterdam (see also pp.151, 166, 173). The foreign names of the streets also contribute to this feeling and his efforts to make them familiar are pathetic. When he comes across a street name which sounds Jewish and vaguely familiar, his joy is out of all proportion. He regards it as 'something close to him and in some obscure way belonging to him, just as though he himself belonged to this street' (p.151). Deprived of his home, Meir desperately tries to adopt the street in which his hotel is located by constantly studying the map of Amsterdam and familiarising himself with the immediately surrounding streets. In an attempt to become intimate with it he drops the word 'street' after its name, as he used to do with the streets of Tel Aviv, and refers to it as Rokin: 'and he returned to Rokin, here he felt at home' (p.182). All his pathetic problems involved in finding a room in the hotel express his fears: 'It was very hard for him, almost impossible to do his sightseeing without knowing that he had a specific place which was his own. It aroused a sense of uprootedness and restlessness which broke the little will and strength which he still had left in him for seeing and absorbing' (p.144). Meir is disappointed to realise that he is probably regarded by the locals as just as much a foreigner as an Asian or an African tourist. Yet, naively he thinks that this is unjustified because he considers himself closer than they are to Europe and to European culture:

> After all he was an engineer and he studied history, including the history of Holland, or in any case the history of Europe, and he read books, 'Til Eulenspiegel', and he admired the paintings of Rembrandt and Breugel and others; and that is not to speak of the great sympathy which he felt for the Dutch and which they felt for Israel. (p.173)

As his mental and physical conditions deteriorate, the descriptions of Amsterdam become similar to the descriptions of Tel Aviv and, in the same automatic and mechanical manner, Amsterdam is projected as empty and desolate (p.184). There are fewer and fewer features that distinguish the two places from one another and, despite the repetitive itineraries, the reader cannot conjure up visions of Amsterdam any more than of Tel Aviv. Here too the focus shifts from the outer world to the inner world of the protagonist. Although he records every minute detail of Amsterdam, it is as if all these details were perceived through a barrier and he were 'unable fully to reach them and sense their real essence' (p.142). Paradoxically, the apparent familiarity of the place emphasises Meir's sense of alienation and detachment from it. Here again, the descriptions of the place are used by the author not just to reflect the protagonist's mood, but to actualise his emotional and physical state:

> A heavy, unpleasant silence hung in the moist air, and a dense smell of standing water and dampness and mildew, but he did not stop and as if chased he increased the pace of his walk and its agitated determination, the green bag pressing on his shoulder badly, he crossed the small wooden bridge, which was revealed at the last minute, and he entered a very narrow alleyway. From the moment he took a few steps in this alleyway with its gloomy wall of houses on both sides, he knew that he had made a terrible mistake and that it would be better to return and go along the street, by the canal, and now he felt even more trapped than before. (pp.134–5)

Meir leaves Amsterdam for London in the third chapter. He is optimistic and excited with the prospect of moving to a new place but the reader is by now fully aware that a change of location will not change anything. Thus, the poetic function of place is different in this chapter: it recedes to the background, on both the thematic and structural levels of the text. London serves only as a setting to the central theme of the chapter, which is the inner thoughts of a sick man, who is progressing towards death far away from home. Meir's first impressions of London are as enthusiastic as those of Amsterdam. After all, he has visited London once before and he can speak the language. Nevertheless, he feels just as much of a stranger and this makes him even more homesick than before. He perceives London only in terms of tourists' sights and, once again, the reader is unable to recreate an authentic view of the place.

Of his tragic collapse at the well-known Foyles bookshop, Meir is most upset that it should happen 'in such a strange place among such strange people' (p.191), but as he regresses into the 'bubble' which separates him from the outside world, the feeling of alienation matters less and less. That the final stages of this regression take place in a bookshop is significant: the motif of books is important in the general scheme of characterisation, as Baruch Link points out.[16] Many books and names of authors appear throughout (including Shabtai's own *Past Continuous*), and who reads what has great meaning. Of particular interest is the description of the legendary Sargasso Sea from *The Bermuda Triangle*, mentioned in the first chapter of *Past Perfect*. The sea is associated with the death of Meir's mother as well as with his own illness. Eventually it transpires that the sea has become a metaphor for the protagonist's deteriorating state and his fear of death.

After Meir's return home, the actual place – Tel Aviv – hardly exists. In the realm between life and death Meir evokes people and places which have shaped his consciousness. In his hallucinatory state he sees only the open countryside and no longer Tel Aviv. It is as if, Nissim Calderon has observed, 'all the places where he has been to, and those which he would have liked to have been to, are joined into one imagined place, and all the different times of his life are joined into one point in time, a point where time disappears'.[17] As the themes of illness and death increase in the story, the role of the actual place where he is – Tel Aviv – decreases: the lack of real place descriptions is as clear an indication of Meir's present state as their earlier elaboration was of his earlier state.

The place serves not only as the background against which the plot and the characters are set, but also as a poetic device to characterise and analyse the protagonist, for place images can reveal a psychic state. This is not just the Romantic strategy of using nature to reflect human moods, but nature taken as an extension of the very make-up of the characters. Consequently, the focus shifts from the external space to the internal space of consciousness. As Gershon Shaked wrote: 'the Jewish writer always exposes the vantage point rather than the object of his observation'.[18] To conclude, place in this novel and its presentation in dialectical terms of home and abroad, or of outside and inside, is used primarily as a poetic tool to analyse the human soul, contrary to the reader's expectations: its images reveal the protagonist's psychic and physical state.

NOTES

1. 'Tamar Meroz interviews Edna Shabtai', in *Modern Hebrew Literature* (Institute for Translation of Hebrew Literature), 3:4 (Spring/Summer 1985), Vol. 10, pp.12–15.
2. Edna Shabtai, *Vaharei 'at* (*For Love is Strong as Death*) (Jerusalem: Keter, 1986), p.68.
3. See Stephen W. Hawking, *A Brief History of Time* (London: Bantam, 1988), p.34.
4. Quotations from the Book of Ecclesiastes are from the King James Version.
5. All translations are my own and are literal rather than literary. For a fine English translation, by Dalya Bilu, see the Viking Penguin 1987 edition.
6. See pp.13, 15, 18, 38, 48, 55, 61, 67, 116, 132, 137, 140, 156, 164, 165, 168, 176, 180, 185, 186, 189, 192, 193, 194, 196, 199, 206, 207, 208, 218, 225, 227, 230, 231.
7. Yitzhak Oren, *Hatzda'ah lasifrut ha-Yisra'elit* (*Salute to Israeli Literature*) (Rishon Letzion: Yahad, 1991), pp.98–105.
8. Ortsion Bartana, *Lavo heshbon* (*To Call to Account*) (Tel Aviv: Alef, 1985), pp.94–5.
9. Dagobert Runes (ed.), *Dictionary of Philosophy* (London: Peter Owen, 1972), p.297.
10. See pp.19, 32, 39, 40, 66, 95, 105, 113.
11. Wolfgang Iser, 'The Reading Process: A Phenomenological Approach', in Jane P. Tompkins (ed.), *Reader-Response: From Formalism to Post-Structuralism* (Baltimore and London: Johns Hopkins University Press, 1981), p.62.
12. See Edna Shabtai, 'Tel Aviv baproza shel Ya'akov Shabtai' ('Tel Aviv in the Prose of Yaakov Shabtai'), *Ah'shav 56* (Spring/Summer 1991), pp.54–78).
13. Cited in Mary Lynn Broe and Angela Ingram (eds), *Women's Writing in Exile* (Chapel Hill and London: University of North Carolina Press, 1989), p.2.
14. Yitzhak Orpaz, *Hatzalian hahiloni* (*The Secular Pilgrim*) (Tel Aviv: Hakibbutz Hameuchad, 1982), p.18.
15. Gershon Shaked, *Lelo motza* (*Dead End*) (Tel Aviv: Hakibbutz Hameuchad, 1973), p.58.
16. Baruch Link, 'Liheyot Italki! . . . Liheyot meshorer!' ('To be Italian! . . . To be a Poet!'), *Alei siach 26* (Tel Aviv: Hachugim Lesifrut, 1989), pp.11–17.
17. Nissim Calderon, *Hargasha shel makom* (*A Sense of Place*) (Tel Aviv: Hakibbutz Hameuchad, 1988), p.40.
18. See the whole passage in Shaked, op. cit., pp.54–65.

2

Molcho

by A. B. YEHOSHUA

The title of this novel, which is the surname of the male protagonist, discloses one of its main rhetorical strategies – that of
alienation – and one of its central themes – oriental Jews.
Molcho is the name of a sixteenth-century Kabbalist and
pseudo-messiah, whose sermons were filled with the expecta-
tion of a coming redemption. Later adopted by oriental Jews, it
became a fairly common surname. To use the protagonist's surname only, never his first name, reveals at the outset the alienation and distance with which he is going to be viewed. To use
it in the title emphasises that the protagonist is of oriental origin. Indeed, he is identified as such by another oriental character in the story, who regards him as 'one of us' on hearing his
surname.[1] This Molcho's struggles are different from those of
his historical counterpart, but both Molchos wanted redemption: the contemporary Molcho tries to redeem himself from
the cultural and social domination of his Ashkenazi wife. The
choice of title suggests that the protagonist stands for something beyond the personal and particular, that he is also symbolic (corroborated as one reads by the extensive use of symbols
throughout the novel).

Molcho was born in Jerusalem, an only child to religious
Sephardi parents, who never went further than Tel Aviv
(p.145).[2] He is 51 years old, a little heavy, with grey curly hair
and dark eyes.[3] His German-born wife has just died of cancer
after seven years of prolonged suffering. The couple had been
married for 30 years and had three grown-up children, as well
as each having an elderly mother.[4] The story unfolds with the
cyclical rhythm of the changing seasons: there are five chapters
in the novel, each corresponding to a season. The fifth season
stands as both a metaphor and a hope for everything which

remains after death, emphasising that to explore beyond the obvious is a central idea of the novel. It has been suggested that the seasons are analogous to a symphony: the two autumns are like the 'exposition' and the 'rephrasing' of a symphony, and the remaining seasons are like the 'development' sections.[5] Each chapter focuses on Molcho's relationship with a different woman, all of which are doomed to fail. Autumn (pp.11–75), significantly, is associated with Molcho's wife and her death; winter (pp.79–127) with the legal adviser from his office in Haifa; spring (pp.131–82) with an 11-year-old girl from a remote settlement in the Galilee; summer (pp.185–263) with an old schoolfriend of his from Jerusalem, and the second autumn (pp.267–346) with a new immigrant who defects back to Russia. The second and fifth chapters take place abroad and the others take place in Israel against the background of the Israeli evacuation of Lebanon in the early 1980s (p.144).

The story is narrated in the third person but is presented from Molcho's point of view. This is evident from both the stance of the narration and the linguistic style. The style here is on the whole colourless, insignificant and apposite to a sophisticated or intellectual standpoint. It matches Molcho's character whilst distancing the reader from him. It creates the gap required for irony, sarcasm and alienation. This distance is enforced by the fact that some of the characters' names are not introduced until much later in the story (and by the use of the protagonist's surname only, as we have seen).[6]

Furthermore, there is no use of inverted commas for direct speech, once again creating an effect of distance. The extensive use of paratactically structured sentences brings together Molcho's fragmented thoughts into one unit of time (for example, pp.11, 38, 44). It also enables the author to direct the reader away from the dominant voice to the minor ones – all of which are different aspects of the same character.[7]

Death and illness are the themes which open and close the novel, and whose presences are strongly felt throughout.[8] Molcho is obsessed by them. He describes them in detailed, clinical terms, at times detached, at others totally absorbed; attracted and at the same time repulsed by them. For him, death is concrete, 'like the black and rough iron ball which they used to bring to gym classes at the forecourt of High School' (p.12).

It is ugly and, tragically, so final (for example, pp.16, 59, 163). His obsession manifests itself through pathetic and excessive repetitions of his concern for his own bodily functions, such as constantly mentioning the need to urinate, to check his stools for blood (for example, pp.12, 15, 19, 21, 64), or through the need to talk about illness and his desire to look after the sick. He served as a male nurse in the army, which is where he first met his wife (p.82). His renewed relationship with Ya'ara, his old schoolfriend from Jerusalem, centres on her constant need to be looked after. The unborn babies she has miscarried fascinate him. The only situation in which he feels comfortable with the legal adviser is after she has fallen down. When he has to look after her, he is on familiar ground. This is reminiscent of his relationship with his wife and her illness, when he was in full control of her life. And so he feels at home in the German pharmacy, among familiar bottles and labels (p.179), and in other peoples' bathrooms where he can glimpse the different medications. The descriptions of the physical deformity of his wife resulting from the cancer, of the different apparatus and medication required during the last stages of her terrible illness, are all given in a cold and factual manner. This detachment in fact reflects a great deal of courage. Molcho crosses a fine line of social convention, which prohibits any overt display of interest in death: to the embarrassment of most, he enjoys telling everyone about the last few weeks before her death. In so doing, as has been suggested elsewhere, he also manages to familiarise himself, as well as the reader, with cancer and thereby make it less threatening: 'He took it out, as it were, from the agonising oncological departments of hospitals and placed it on a lofty, knightly bed hovering like a ship in the homely bedroom.'[9] Through his protagonist, Yehoshua bravely looks at death itself and compels the hedonistic reader to join him and to confront it squarely.

Molcho's reading of Tolstoy's *Anna Karenina* during the whole year gives death an extra dimension. The Russian novel counter-mirrors our novel: it ends shortly after the death of the protagonist, whereas our novel begins shortly before; Anna Karenina committed suicide when she lost her freedom, whilst Molcho re-enters life when he regains his. The old eternal triangle on which the Russian story depends operates in Molcho except that one member of the triangle is dead. Yet the dead wife's presence prevents a liaison between Molcho and any other woman. It is ironic that Molcho is disappointed with the last part of *Anna Karenina*, 'wondering what had prevented the author from simply ending it after the death of the heroine' (p.297), since much of Yehoshua's novel is preoccupied with what happens after someone dies: it suggests that in real life, as in fiction, all is not lost with death. This idea is also conveyed on the metaphoric level of the text: Yehoshua presents the private relationship of Molcho with his wife, her illness and her death as a metaphor for the public ailing Israeli society. The country is overtly compared to a sick person. When Molcho's family gather for one of their ritual Friday night meals, 'they moaned a bit about the country, but without special excitement, as if already moaning about a dying person' (p.53). The remote and impoverished settlement in the Galilee, inhabited by oriental immigrants, seems to be disintegrating 'like an incurably sick man' (p.167–8). Susan Sontag observed that

> Illnesses have always been used as metaphors to enliven charges that a society was corrupt or unjust. . . . They are used to propose new, critical standards of individual health, and to express a sense of dissatisfaction with society as such. Unlike the Elizabethan metaphors – which complain of some general aberration or public calamity that is, in consequence, dislocating to individuals – the modern metaphors suggest a profound disequilibrium between individual and society, with society conceived as the individual's adversary. Disease metaphors are used to judge society not as out of balance but repressive.[10]

One of the social conditions which Yehoshua examines is the effects of the superior attitude of Ashkenazi Jews, who impose their European culture on the whole society. They are driven by pride and prejudice, just like the protagonists of Jane Austen's novel with that title, which Molcho also reads. Yehoshua observes that the creative forces of oriental Jews are frustrated as a result of this superior attitude, which causes their intellectual impotence. Molcho's life epitomises this frustration and subservience. He sacrificed his whole existence, at first to please and then to tend to his wife. His employers at the Ministry of Interior accommodated his domestic problems and gave him exemption from adhering strictly to office hours – no doubt this halted his professional progress. He was determined, at great financial, physical and emotional cost, to fulfil his wife's wish to die with dignity in her own home. He was supportive, tender, and assisted in every possible way to alleviate her pains and help retain her dignity. He lovingly accepted the fact that for seven years he was denied a sex life, had to give up smoking, and had to attend to all domestic chores, including dyeing her hair. (These seven years allude to the Bible, where Jacob had to work for seven years before he could marry his beloved Rachel.) Molcho did not even allow himself to be unwell during his wife's illness. His attempts to draw sympathy from the cleaning lady and from his mother-in-law, when he allows himself to succumb to being unwell after the death, are pathetic. He enjoys all the attention poured on him during the funeral and the seven days of mourning. It reassures him that no one really blames him for her death. Yet, with all his enormous and selfless efforts, Molcho does feel guilty. He worries that the family doctor might hold him responsible for the death, an accusation which is actually voiced by the legal adviser later in the novel. This absurd sense of guilt is the natural feeling of a surviving partner, but it also reveals Molcho's deep inferiority complex.

It is because of this inferiority complex that Molcho makes continuous and ridiculous efforts to impress others and to be liked by them (for example, pp.21, 24, 43). He is proud that his devotion to his wife is renowned, and does not want to risk his reputation by being seen at a concert during his year of mourning, regardless of how much he wants to hear music. He is pleased to notice that not only close colleagues from his office have come to the funeral, but also many secretaries and caretakers. These people must have come because they like or respect him, but he himself does not recognise this possibility. It comes as a surprise to discover that he holds a fairly senior position in his office (p.251). He enjoys the visits by the consoling neighbours, even though he knows that they have really come to cry 'their own private cry' (p.21). Pathetically, he enjoys the 'new style of kissing' (p.25) even though he is aware that it is the proximity to death and sickness which attracts most people to him and not his own real self.

The stance of inferiority is emphasised by Molcho's ridiculous reverence to his mother-in-law's old-age home. He regards the place as a haven of culture, where everyone, including the driver, speaks German (for example, pp.34, 52, 66, 259). His close relationship with his mother-in-law stems from his admiration of her being so cultured, well read and well presented. He respects her pride and her independence, and he looks after her with the same sense of servitude he had shown his wife. It is only towards her death at the end of the novel that Molcho succeeds in shaking off his inferiority complex and feels sufficiently liberated to refer to her as 'the wife's mother' (p. 307) instead of 'the old lady'. Molcho's mother, on the other hand, stands in contrast to the European lady. She is fat, heavily made-up and unsophisticated. He phones her daily and she always nags him about food and tells him what to do and how to behave. Yet all her concerns about her only child, irritating though they are, seem more 'normal' and more natural than the controlled behaviour of his wife and her mother. Although Molcho's mother is much more integrated in Israeli life and has many more friends and relatives, she is afraid of the two women and feels inferior. After the death she hopes that her son will at last find a woman who will be 'closer to his blood' (p.137), and that he will not have to change his ways so much. Even before his wife's illness it was Molcho who had to adapt himself to her cultural and social codes of behaviour, rather than the other way around. During her illness Molcho was so preoccupied with her that he afterwards decides that he has to train his brain to think again. But he knows that she always had the sharper intellect (p.125) and when he was either with her or with the legal adviser, who resembles her very much, he felt that he was slow and unoriginal (p.91).

The oriental Jews, like Molcho, are anxious to acquire European culture. Through him, his wife accused the orientals of neglecting issues of equal importance, such as formulating their own attitude to a political ideology. It seemed to her that this was one of the contributory reasons for the backward state in which they found themselves. Whilst Molcho admits to himself on several occasions that he is not an intellectual, the shallow and pretentious intellectual interests of the Ashkenazi relations of the legal adviser, for example, are presented critically. He does not notice that the fireplace in her flat is a mock one, but it is she who chose to have a reproduction in the first place. Similarly, Molcho discovers only after his wife's death that most of their friends are in fact unoriginal and plain boring (p.42). Their preoccupation with intellectual matters distracts them from appreciating nature, for example (p.140). The question is whether Ashkenazi culture is a worthy model to imitate, at the expense of the Sephardi community losing its own vitality and identity. Yehoshua's negative answer is firm, but he forecasts that a new and healthier future might be possible only after the death of the domination of Ashkenazi culture, which is analogous to the death of Molcho's Ashkenazi wife. Thus, he suggests that death can have an important purifying effect. Throughout the novel, death is associated with rain, a symbol which traditionally signifies purification[11] and whose positive effects were felt by Molcho: 'it is as if it came only to purify the air' (p.17).[12]

Tragic though death is, it grants freedom to the two partners of a marriage: freedom to the one who departs from a life full of suffering, and freedom to the one still living. However, Yehoshua warns that the freedom can be obtained only when the survivors rid themselves of the influence of the dead, something which Molcho admits is not easy: 'For the dead don't really disappear' (p.314). Although his wife's constant criticism of him has ceased, he is so conditioned to it that he finds it hard not to continue to abide by it (pp.139, 158, 310, 331). As if brainwashed, he still continues to shower and change his clothes too often, whilst as a child he bathed only once a week. He is now conditioned to worry about cleanliness, tidiness, or eating non-oily food, all of which he acquired through years of living with his German-born wife. Yosef Oren has observed that

> the novel mocks at Molcho, who lost his masculine identity because of a youthful folly, when he fell for the European bespectacled blond, the intellectual woman, whose principles and ideology have uprooted him from life. . . . The novel protests against the tyranny of an ideology which was conceived in exilic Europe under entirely different circumstances, and against its utopic demands. . . . It seems that this is how Yehoshua understands the quality of normality of the state of Israel: a state which solves its problems according to sane possibilities rather than according to pretentious utopias of impractical ideology. The novel calls for another Zionism, for Zionism which compromises with life and which blends with the oriental space in which the state is joined. In order to facilitate life, it is permitted to divorce an outdated ideology. It is permitted to divorce it and to depart from it, despite its great virtues. Despite the fact that it aroused the revolution of national revival for one hundred years, which established a state now entering its fortieth year.[13]

Molcho's wife was a bitter woman who was hard to please and could never be fully happy (p.126). She was very critical of herself, as well as of others, and her judgement was as harsh about private issues as public ones (p.139). She was involved with political debates and held strong and uncompromising views. She vehemently opposed the religious parties in Israel and the unfair imposition of their ideology on the rest of the population (p.199), as well as the Israeli invasion of Lebanon. She refused ever to visit Germany on principle, though her refusal might have been linked to the fact that her father had committed suicide there. Molcho's wife had been the active partner in their marriage, and even when very sick she had still made the decisions about the furniture arrangements in the house, her menu, and how she was to be looked after in her sickness (p.29). In a very down-to-earth manner she had chosen their flat according to the view she would have from the window when on her death bed, and advised her husband on his remarriage after her death. Although eight or nine years previously she had left home for a day or two (p. 134), and although Molcho knew that he irritated her at times, their marriage seems to have been a solid one. They developed the intimate habits of people reconciled to spending their life together (for example, pp.274, 311).

During her illness, when sex no longer played a part in their life, a deep compassion replaced it (p. 33). Mid-life crisis is no doubt one of the contributing factors for Molcho's impotence, but loyalty and devotion to his wife are others. He cannot arouse his dormant desires whilst still under her spell. The presence of the young cleaning lady, the photographs of naked women or the physical warmth of the bodies of the young women soldiers to whom he offers a lift cannot arouse him, however hard he tries (pp.86, 91, 145). It is ironic that the only occasion he is vaguely successful is when he is absurdly attracted to the 11-year-old Cochin girl from Zeru'a, possibly because he knows that their relationship could not be fulfilled.[14] He puts it down to his primal sexual, bestial instincts which he realises with relief are doomed to be sublimated:

> And Molcho, his hunger increasing, kept looking at the little round bottom moving about assertively in front of him, behind the tight black material of her leotard. He kept on looking at the slim girl who was leading him with proud yet gentle firmness, and kept on thinking to himself, why does she attract me so, as if she had burst into my soul. It is sheer madness. And suddenly a bestial thought had seized him, a kind of primal sexual thought, that he could have eaten her up, chewed her flesh, and his teeth chattered a little and the thought made him laugh a little, but also frightened him and depressed him. (p.152)

44

Many of his suppressed desires are diverted to food. When he finds himself in a more plausible situation with the Russian woman, he still cannot betray the memory of his wife, and he gives himself the naive excuse that 'to lie without really talking is a bestial act' (p.311). Consequently, his conclusion, which closes the novel, is that 'one has to fall really in love' (p.346). This is his only hope in order to liberate himself and obtain his freedom.

Molcho's obsession with classical music is another example of the effect of Ashkenazi brainwashing. Music had been very important to his wife, who died to the sound of Mahler. At the close of the novel Molcho wants her mother also to die to the sound of music by the very same composer, on a cassette given to her by Molcho – but she doesn't want to listen to it. After his wife's death, Molcho has to re-examine his own attitude to music, rather than just follow her love for it. Although his knowledge of music is very basic,[15] he loves it so passionately that he finds it difficult not to go to concerts during the year of mourning. Music, of course, is one way of communicating with his dead wife, but it also genuinely excites him and 'melted the dead cells within him' (p.81). Whereas the legal adviser and her relatives conceive of music in intellectual terms, he responds to it emotionally. The question is whether the instinctive reaction of the unsophisticated Sephardi is, in fact, inferior to the more cultivated and intellectual reaction of the Ashkenazi. The use of irony suggests that it is not necessarily inferior.

After his wife's death, Molcho discovers operas, and their drama assumes a special significance in his life. When he visits Berlin he goes to hear *Don Giovanni*, the hero of which is the epitome of the sexual seducer, but by mistake he finds himself listening to Gluck's *Orpheus and Eurydice*. Instead of finding a man acting Don Juan, he finds a woman acting as a man. This is another allusion to the feminine aspects of Molcho's personality.[16] He discovers that in addition to his affinity to Orpheus, there are major events in his own life similar to those of the opera. He realises that he too has acted in a tragic drama, in which he himself was 'such an obedient protagonist' (p.113). He begins to view his own life as a drama, with himself on stage and the people around him his audience. Furthermore, through his musical skills, Orpheus succeeds in entering hell in search of his beloved dead wife. Similarly, Molcho feels that he reaches his dead wife through music. But, whilst Orpheus employs music in order to redeem his wife, Molcho uses it to redeem himself. There are other allusions in the novel to this opera, and the lengthy description of it suggests its importance in understanding the text. It has been pointed out that the idea of hell is as central to the novel as it is to the opera.[17] Hell in *Molcho* is repeatedly presented symbolically in different guises: as the wadis in Haifa and in the Galilee; the deep, dark beer cellar; the dark mausoleum; the stage of the opera, which looks like an abyss; the cellar in Germany where Molcho stores the possessions of the Russian defector, and many more.

Music helps Molcho exorcise his wife's hold on him, and it is only after his return from his opera trip to Germany that he is no longer compelled to be as passionate about music as he has been before. On his second visit he is liberated enough to divert his attention from the music itself to the director of the opera. Towards the close of the novel, Molcho joins a tour of the old opera house in East Berlin where, after farcically being mistaken for Siegfried, he feels free to run away from the opera and from music.

Altogether his wife's death liberates Molcho from his heavy responsibilities and gives him a new kind of freedom (pp.17, 27, 40, 84, 102). His attitude towards it fluctuates. At times he tries to convince himself that it is exciting: 'he walked about with a kind of a new freedom, knowing that from now on he was not bound by anything' (p.17; also pp.27, 102, 269). Yet at others he is scared by it (p.84), realising its negative consequences: 'There are those who are undoubtedly envious of his new freedom and do not grasp how difficult loneliness sometimes is' (p.40; also p.34). He does not know what to do with this freedom. Ironically, after so many years of marriage and servitude, freedom seems more like fetters. His constant preoccupation with practical matters manifests a desperate attempt to fill the vacuum in his life. During his wife's illness, Molcho was the one who attended to all family matters, even though she controlled them. After her death he continues to do so, with an outburst of feverish urgency. Molcho may still be influenced by his dead wife's calculating attitude to money (p. 50), but his concern for practical matters reflects his loneliness. Immediately after her death he rearranges their bedroom and bathroom, which had been her domain during her illness, returns the medical equipment no longer needed, and tries to sell the remaining expensive medication. These attempts assume ridiculous proportions (p.58). Indeed, most of his activities are directed towards saving money. When he is with the legal adviser in Germany, he tries to avoid a situation in which he would have to pay for her meal, and when he has to buy her a bandage, he makes sure that it is the cheapest. When he goes to Europe with the Russian woman, he takes the remaining apples from home, rather than waste them (p.274). He makes sure that there will be no waste of electricity or food in his house, and that the claim for the last part of his wife's salary as well as for the last payment of the German reparation should not be forgotten. The fact that his profession is accountancy does not sufficiently explain his obsession with calculations. The author details all Molcho's boring, mundane engagements and the endless precise lists of his expenses, to such an extent that the reader tires of it and loses sympathy for him.

He begins to cook regularly and sees diligently to all the domestic chores. All these activities are presented as despicable. Yet, no doubt, readers will be able to identify at least some of these obsessions in themselves. We are given an insight into Molcho's petty behaviour, which in no way contradicts the sincerity or depth of his inner emotions towards his dead wife, but shows an almost animal instinct for survival, which prevails even at a time of extreme grief. His desperate attempts to arouse his sexual instincts by the chance touch of a woman's breast, or at the mere sight of the legal adviser, are not to be seen as examples of disloyalty to the memory of his wife. This is an existential reaction to the danger incurred by emotional disturbance. Yehoshua acknowledges this phenomenon and bravely portrays the hidden, ugly aspects of the human being, at the risk of alienating the protagonist from the reader. This is why the reader sways between sympathy and repulsion for Molcho. But, despite his obsessive and tiresome pettiness, despite the mediocrity of his character, Molcho emerges as a real hero. He is able to confront death and to come to terms with it as an inevitable part of life. More than that, he manages to liberate himself from the influence of the dead.

Place

Descriptions of the landscape in Israel are rather scant in this novel. Molcho's horizons do not extend beyond his home-town Haifa, his birth-town Jerusalem, and the two settlements in the Galilee which he visits during the course of the story. In Haifa, the dominant feature is the wadi which can be seen from his flat. Its depth is conceived as an 'abyss', which is usually identified with the land of the dead, the underworld. The accumulation of symbols associated with hell and the abyss calls for attention. The proximity of the wadi to the flat was one of the determining factors in purchasing the flat. The wadi's appearance changes according to the time of the day, the time of the year and according to Molcho's moods. At times it seems to him as if after her death, his wife has disappeared into the mysterious darkness of the wadi (for example, p.39). At others, especially in the spring, the wadi appears sensuously attractive to him, filled with trees and shrubs growing in the moist soil, and is described with heavy sexual overtones (for example, pp.44, 132). It is in God-forsaken Zeru'a that he discovers another deep wadi with thick vegetation, and to which he once again finds himself almost sexually attracted. The strong smells of the shrubs arouse his senses and, again, the terminology used to describe the wadi is loaded with sexual connotations (p.165). It is enough for our purpose to say that the wadi clearly signifies something beyond its literal meaning, that it becomes a symbol, or a leitmotif. Juxtaposed with the wadis, which are symbolically situated in the lower zone of any given landscape, we have the high mountains of Haifa, the Galilee and of Jerusalem. We mainly know of the heights from Molcho's trips to the north.

The only ordinary levels of the landscape are abroad, in Paris, Berlin and Vienna.

There are brief prosaic descriptions of the urban features of Haifa, a stronghold of the German cultured bourgeoisie community: Molcho's undistinguished apartment block standing on its stilts, the legal adviser's ugly 1960s apartment block with its typically neglected garden and visible rubbish bins (p.47); a new supermarket in his neighbourhood; a few shops and crowded beaches. Even when he wants to boast to his old schoolfriend Ya'ara and her husband Uri about the beautiful view from the university campus, he cannot do so because the vision is blurred by the hot summer air. Desperate to impress them with the place, he compares Jerusalem to Haifa, expressing his preference for the latter, but with little enthusiasm and conviction (p.227). Only the Bahai Temple really impresses him, but that is because it is outside the normal realm of Israeli landscape, and it reminds him of abroad (p.223). Only after his return from abroad is Molcho able to admit that after all the years he has lived in Haifa, he is in fact an 'uprooted' man. He then begins to be able to see his surroundings clearly, as if after a blinding disease: 'When he would come down the green slope of Stella Maris, the horizon opened up with a sweep, up to the white rock of Rosh Hanikrah, and the coastline was cut into details in a secured and precise sharpness, whilst keeping the soft roundness of the bay' (p.267). On the rare occasions that Molcho visits his mother in Jerusalem, he only notices the shabbiness of Jaffa Street and the narrow alleyways of Mahaneh-Yehudah market, and he manages to have only a vague glimpse of the mountains, through the toilet window. (It is from the same undignified spot that he sees the summit of Mount Hermon when he is in Zeru'a: p.152.)

In general, Yehoshua only isolates certain facets of places in Israel in order to expose social discontent and to criticise them. For example, apart from the geographical height of Kibbutz Yodefet, the stagnating social state of its members is emphasised and associated with the memories of Ya'ara's many miscarriages. Similarly, when Molcho visits Zeru'a, the features of 'place' which are described are the social deterioration, the mis-

erable living conditions of its oriental inhabitants and the ubiq-
uitous neglect. Yehoshua uses place to offer his social criticism
of the Israeli establishment which forsakes the poor immigrants
and leaves them to struggle with a hopeless and corrupt bureau-
cracy. The description of the new orthodox neighbourhood,
where Ya'ara and Uri live in Jerusalem, serves to express
Yehoshua's criticism of the ultra orthodox communities in
Israel. Although he is sympathetic to secular Israelis who turn
to anarchic orthodoxy, such as Ya'ara and Uri, he is critical of
the majority who continue to conduct their life as if they were
still living in the eastern Europe they had left behind, unaffected by the secular state in which they actually live. Molcho is
amazed when he visits one of their neighbourhoods:

> and it was as if they had left behind the dark and
> somewhat desolate Jerusalem, and arrived at another
> city which at that late hour of night was full of life,
> with scores of small lights, as if it were a big power
> station. . . . Now they . . . climbed a few steps to the
> entrance of one of the buildings, crowded with tod-
> dlers and several pregnant women. . . . and so they
> stood waiting for the lift, also full of children, which
> obviously stopped at every level. Indeed when the lift
> arrived and the door opened many toddlers escaped
> from it with joyful shrieks. . . . And so the lift stopped
> on every floor and the children came and went. On
> every floor Molcho saw doors of flats opened and
> people moving about . . . and he was filled with such
> a sharp sense of life that it gave him a slight fright.
> (pp.195–6)

Yehoshua warns us implicitly that such 'black' (strictly orthodox) areas, where Jews live outside the boundaries of normal
statehood, are dangerous to the Israeli state.

On the whole, places in Israel are perceived as ordinary and
undistinguished, corresponding to Molcho's character. The
analogy established between the landscape and Molcho's ordi-
nariness is based on similarity. Shlomith Rimmon-Kenan has
termed it a 'straight' analogy, reinforcing the characterisation.[18]

It enhances the reader's perception of a certain trait of Molcho's character only after it has already been revealed through his actions, speech and appearance. The problems of determining literal and 'straight' meanings are not necessarily less difficult than finding those of figurative ones.

Against this treatment of places in Israel, let us examine the treatment of places abroad. Before the wife's death the couple had been abroad several times, and they had particularly liked visiting her cousin and husband in Paris. Despite these trips, Molcho has to admit that 'I am an old Sephardi, fifth generation in Israel, and Europe is still strange to us' (p.68). Nevertheless, after his wife's death he decides to go to Paris again, and this time he agrees to stay at the cousins' tiny flat, a departure from the pattern set by his wife. The freezing January weather, and particularly the snow, dominates his visit. Clearly the cold weather is no more dominant in Paris than the scorching heat of the summer in Haifa. The change of time, weather, season, and even place, seem to have no effect on Molcho's existence. The separate units of the text do not stop the linear progression of the story, but rather string it together.[19] Thoughts about his wife dominate Molcho in Paris just as much as they do in Haifa. He walks about the city visiting what used to be their favourite places, and even goes on a tour to Versaille. He cannot enjoy it because he is thinking about his wife's death and his unwanted new freedom. He spends most of the time chatting with the cousins and helping them with mundane chores such as shopping and collecting their child from his nursery school. At a restaurant, the cousins 'questioned him about the situation in Israel and about the country's prospects in general; the doctor repeatedly asked, with a kind of inexplicable annoyance, do you Israelis want to commit suicide? And Molcho tried to explain whatever he could. I don't understand much in politics, he confessed at last' (p.80). This off-hand comment, interjected casually into the general description of the evening, says much more than at first appears. Yehoshua relies more on what is not said than on what is said. When abroad, Molcho reacts to the internal affairs of Israel in the same way as he would do were he back home. The distance does not seem to make it easier for him to reflect about himself and his life in a more detached way. The major event of his visit to Paris is his decision to go to an opera for the first time in his life. It is as if 'a craze for operas has emerged out of his wife's death' (p.84), and at great expense he treats the cousins to hear Mozart's *The Magic Flute*. Under the pretext of this new thirst for operas, Molcho goes to Berlin, where place assumes different dimensions in the structure of the text.

When Molcho first arrives in Berlin he has preconceived ideas about it, mainly associated with his wife and her cultured German background. The reader is reminded that the impressions of place in the novel are subjective, presented from the protagonist's viewpoint. Molcho's initial impression is of Berlin's cultural atmosphere: 'The streets looked quiet and cultured' (p. 85). Any Hebrew reader of the twentieth century reacts to Germany with caution. When Wagner's music, which is played on the flight from Paris, does not arouse any uncomfortable feelings in Molcho, the reader is alerted. A gap is created between the reader and the protagonist. For the Jewish reader, Wagner and Germany are associated with Nazism. Yet Molcho does not think of the place in terms of the Holocaust. Naively, or worse still, through ignorance, he considers Germany a 'neutral' place, suitable for liberating himself from the memory of his wife and for pursuing his affair with the legal adviser. His first thought is that he has never been to a more northerly spot on the face of the earth. The reddish colour of the sky, the sight of the quaint old quarter of the city and its cleanliness and the homeliness of his hotel are all exciting and welcoming signs. The only hint of unease is the sight of the swords hanging on one of the hotel walls, which the reader associates with Wagner and the legendary Nibelungen German heroes.[20] Molcho refers to the German language heard on the radio with the same indifference as the fact that he is staying in a German hotel, where the German clerk at reception has a little moustache like Hitler's (p.87). No explicit reference is made to the significance of Germany for a visiting Israeli. Only the repetition of the word 'German', culminating with the actual mention of Hitler, spurs the reader to fill the gaps between the explicit and the implicit.

Wolfgang Iser noted in his work on the theory of aesthetic response that the reader

> is drawn into events and made to supply what is meant from what is not said. What is said only appears to take on significance as a reference to what is not said; it is the implications and not the statements that give shape and weight to the meaning. But as the unsaid comes to life in the reader's imagination, so the said 'expands' to take on greater significance than might have been supposed: even trivial scenes can seem surprisingly profound.[21]

Portraying any aspect of the Holocaust in aesthetic terms has been an insurmountable problem for writers. In this novel Yehoshua finds a solution by relying on the reader to supply that which is not said. This unusual poetic use of place is most powerful and effective here. When Molcho meets the legal adviser for the first time in Berlin, he feels 'as if in a bubble outside the world' (p.91), happy to be able to be anonymous. The reader is angered by the fact that Molcho does not even mention that he has walked around Berlin before they meet. Can Molcho, albeit an oriental Jew, arrive in Germany free of the collective memory of the fate of European Jewry? Should any Jew, or indeed any civilised human being, forget this fate? Are there no lessons to be learnt from history? These are some of the questions which are indirectly raised in the text, by their absence. Unlike Molcho, the reader inevitably associates the smoking chimneys on the city's horizon with the chimneys of the concentration camps.

When Molcho enters his hotel room he discovers the New Testament and reads it, probably for the first time, in English. An analogy between Jews and Christians is thus created, and then extended: Molcho imagines that Jerusalem was as full of tension and fear in the time of Jesus as was the Jerusalem of 1948, on the eve of the War of Independence. The bitter irony is that whilst there was much more hope and promise of survival on the eve of the establishment of the new Jewish state than on the eve of the birth of the Christian religion, the latter seems to Yehoshua to have fared better. When Molcho comes across the Berlin Wall, he is reminded of the wall which divided Jerusalem in his youth. Whereas the wall in Jerusalem was a constant threat, the Berlin Wall seems to have given its citizens 'a spot of real tranquillity in the heart of the busy city' (p.113). Although this comparison reveals differences rather than similarities, its implication is nevertheless very disturbing. The suffering of the Germans seems to be light, by comparison.

Placing the protagonist away from home enables Yehoshua to raise these questions of survival from a different perspective, thereby probing deeper into personal and collective existential problems. The excuse for Molcho's trip to Berlin is his meeting with the legal adviser and their visit to the opera. At the opera he is surprised to see the number of young people in the audience, and at their informal dress. This contrasts with the elderly German Jews living in Levantine Israel filling the concert halls, who are – ironically – probably the only remaining Germans to keep the old German tradition. The music Molcho hears is not particularly linked with the place, but rather with his internal emotional state. On the surface level of the text, it seems that the legal adviser's accident, and her subsequent abnormally long and deep sleep, also take the action further away from the actual place. Most of Molcho's time in Berlin is spent on his preoccupation with the sick legal adviser, a situation reminiscent of his wife's illness.[22] The fact that so much of his time is spent on problems unrelated to the place is revealing rather than concealing. Molcho is no more curious to explore Berlin than he was Paris, possibly even less so. In both places he walks in the snow, entering shops and coffee houses, and in neither can he communicate in the spoken language. Every now and again something around him takes him back to Israel, such as the snow, which reminds him of a memorable snowy day in his childhood in Jerusalem. Most of the time he 'flashes back' to his wife and their relationship, yet it is only as an afterthought that Molcho regrets not having taken the address of his wife's childhood home in Berlin. This must be the most likely yet unconscious reason for his visit to the city in the first place. Significantly, juxtaposed to the thought of his wife's childhood in Berlin, he thinks to himself of Hitler: 'perhaps sixty years ago Hitler himself was walking about here, over the same paving stones, gloomy and starving wearing a torn coat, thinking his thoughts of extermination' (p.106). This comment is surreptitiously woven into the text, yet its impact is great. In this context of awakened memory, the chilling images of the church bell ringing in the misty light, and of the elderly barber sitting peacefully in front of his old-fashioned instruments, which might have been used for different haircuts in the concentration camps, send the reader a chilling reminder that perhaps not much has changed. Wanting revenge on the Germans, Molcho decides to have a German haircut and the satisfaction of them serving him, whilst all the time he is thinking to himself: 'Surely they used to be Nazis' (p.114). He may also want to punish himself for not having experienced the concentration camps personally.

The sense of discomfort, tension and above all loneliness overpowers Molcho and he even becomes suspicious of the German germs which may be clinging to the thermometer he has borrowed. His desperate struggles to liberate himself from the hold his dead wife has on him are intertwined with his part in the collective struggle to come to terms with the Holocaust. This must be the main reason why Yehoshua places his protagonist in Germany. On the personal level, Molcho is away from his homeland, alienated and distant from his surroundings, as if 'going into exile' from his home (pp.118–19). Molcho's physical dislocation stands in complete contrast with the German family who own the hotel and the privileged locals who take their evening meals in undisturbed peace and tranquillity (p.117). His visit to Berlin comes to an end in a big beer cellar, where he feels out of place, out of control and in a delirious state, amongst all the jolly people eating and drinking. He feels as if 'the large and tasty sausage which he had eaten reconstituted itself in his stomach and started to crawl inside him, and he felt as if he was on the deck of a large and noisy ship swinging in the waves' (pp.126–7). It is there that he is accused of killing his wife by the legal adviser, and it is there that his relationship with her comes to an end. Strangely, he is pleased to hear her accusation. It has been suggested that the reason for this is that Molcho possesses the instincts of a hunter.[23] Indeed, he calls the legal adviser a 'squirrel', the Russian woman a 'rabbit', and thinks of his wife as a 'hind'. Thus, Molcho's apparent passivity can be interpreted as the tactics of a hunter, patiently lying in wait, and ultimately achieving his goal. He might temporarily be failing in his relationships with women, but ultimately he regains his freedom and hope for future success.

Within a few months of his return to Israel, Molcho goes abroad again and visits Vienna on his way to Berlin. Vienna serves only as a transit stop in the Russian woman's desperate attempt to return to the east. Here too the text relies on what is unsaid. The alienated protagonist does not refer to Vienna explicitly, but as 'the Austrian capital' (p.278) and to the people working at the hotel as 'the Austrians'. The repetition of 'Austrians' alerts the reader not to regard innocently the apparently neutral descriptions, such as this: 'He met Austrians promenading, appearing to him like a kind of lighter and more colourful German, free of a sense of guilt' (pp.294–5). The reader is aware of their collaboration with the Nazis so the statement that they feel guilt-free is shocking. The shock is even stronger because juxtaposed to this apparently neutral remark is the description of the artistic statues in the forest, fine examples of Austrian high culture. Ironically, the only other reference to Vienna's cultural activities is made by the oriental emissary of the Jewish Agency, who lives in an exclusive area, paid for by public Israeli money which should be better spent. Once again, through the description of the place, Yehoshua indirectly offers a social criticism. The only other features of Vienna to be mentioned are unwelcoming: its decadence and the large number of Arab tourists. The reader is called upon to fill the gap in the text and to reflect on the connotations of the Austrian people with the Israelis.

Molcho's second visit to Berlin takes place in a different season and with another woman: the fifth season, in the autumn, when he helps the Russian woman to escape back to Russia. As noted earlier, the fifth season promises a time of hope for that which remains after death. Indeed, after Molcho's absurd mission succeeds, he does manage to exorcise his wife's influence on him. Unlike his first visit to Berlin, during this one he feels immediately at home and is pleased to see the same hotel and its familiar surroundings. He takes his companion along the familiar streets with excitement, passing by familiar shops and the little restaurant. However, this time his feelings for the city are ambivalent. He is pleased to see the buildings which had been destroyed in the war still not fully reconstructed, and to see the Berlin Wall which tears the town apart. To his satisfaction this looks 'like an ugly scar which was being kept meticulously to remind tourists such as himself in a hundred years to come what they would wish to forget' (p.319). Molcho and the Russian woman decide to cross over to East Berlin, where she should find it easier to plead with the authorities to accept her as a defector. The crossing is uneventful and to Molcho's surprise one side of the city seems just like the other: the same boulevards, the same gardens and the same people. Molcho cannot discern the distinction between 'freedom' and 'non-freedom'.

It is only on his second visit to the east the next day that he notices the vast difference between east and west. Everything in East Berlin seems grey, the shops look impoverished and the cars old-fashioned. Again he visits the simple yet moving mausoleum in memory of the victims of the two world wars and nervously he ventures to find his way to his wife's old family home. Sitting on the train he thinks: 'I am in the heart of East Berlin, travelling innocently on the municipal underground, and people around me are ordinary, and it is as if I were one of them' (p.327). On seeing the actual street where his wife used to live, with its little square and swings and some old trees, with its primitive corner shop, he realises how wise she was not to have wanted to come back and revisit this quiet and neglected street. He tries to imagine her as a child in these surroundings and even goes to have a look at a flat in the building where she might have lived. Molcho goes there despite the fact that visiting Germany was against his wife's principles, but it is just there that he shakes off his fear of her and regains his freedom. Whilst the first autumn is associated with death, the second in the cycle is associated with rebirth. Having seen the place of origin of his German-born wife, he no longer walks like a bereaved man, but rather reawakened and as if recovering from an illness. His triumph is personal and also symbolic: it is that of a Sephardi Jew who has not experienced the Holocaust and is therefore made to feel guilty and inferior. It haunts him for years and he has to see for himself the place where the traumatic events of the Ashkenazi community took place. Only by seeing the actual place can he demistify its experience and exorcise its effect on him.

Thus, Molcho's odyssey ends with an optimistic note which is echoed in the closing phrase of the novel: 'one really has to fall in love'. However, as part of the process of recovery, for the time being at least, he is destined to be uprooted and wander about, just like his historical Ashkenazi counterparts, the generation of the 'uprooted' Jews. His flights, both within Israel and abroad, are an inevitable part of the search for his identity. Commenting on this stage of the quest for the self, Hagorni-Green suggests that

> Molcho, like the rest of us, is hovering between here and there. Restlessly. Realism and matter of fact and efficiency and the strength to survive. The need to arrange things. To close matters. To open accounts so that the money should do something in the meantime. . . . To change a car. An alternative to a woman in this case. And at the same time restlessness. To fly away. To rise high in the world. To move about. Hither and thither. As if drugged. . . . The escape from yourself. The search for a borrowed past in order to unite with something stable. To become domesticated. To get rid of foreign currency as if it is the last trip. To bring unnecessary presents. To take part in some sort of crazy ritual. Ceaseless compulsion. To grab. To store. To wander.[24]

Molcho escapes from himself for many years and only wakes up to it after the death of his wife. After all, his self-effacement might be a necessary step in his search for a redefining of his identity. He sought a symbiosis between the Ashkenazi and the Sephardi cultures. His marriage itself was a model for such a symbiosis. He is a Sephardi, his wife was an Ashkenazi, and together they maintained an acceptable *modus vivendi*. Marriage is one of the major themes in this novel and is presented as an important social institution. Molcho's achievement is that he realises that although similar partnerships could be improved, nevertheless they can work. Although he is an unexceptional, dull and boring character, as is the average citizen of any given society, he bravely attempts to assert himself by redefining his identity. Thus, this wandering anti-hero emerges as a hero. I disagree with Ortsion Bartana's conclusion that when Molcho has to cope with his own impotence he fails miserably.[25] On the contrary, after his wife's death, Molcho confronts issues which few Israelis dare to confront. This is Yehoshua's positive, constructive cue for the direction which Israeli society should take. Molcho is not a passive mythical hero, but a hero who faces reality and acts upon it.

NOTES

1. Unless otherwise stated, all translations are my own and are literal rather than literary. An English translation has been published – *Five Seasons* (London: Flamingo, 1990) – but unfortunately I found it wanting. This short quote, for example, is wrongly rendered and the sentence which follows is missing altogether (p.185 in the translation).

2. In an interview with Sarit Fuchs in *Ma'ariv*, 30 Jan. 1987, Yehoshua said that Molcho was modelled after the collector of his father's synagogue, and that it was his father's death which finally stirred him to incorporate his Sephardi past and the theme of death in his novel.

3. Although his precise age is not clear, it is close enough to 50 (see p.41).

4. Dan Laor noted in his book review, 'Bein hametim uvein hahayim' ('Between the Living and the Dead'), *Ha-Aretz*, 27 Feb. 1987, that setting the novel in the framework of a family both continues and extends Yehoshua's two previous novels, *Hame'ahav (The Lover)* and *Gerushim me'uharim (Late Divorce)*.

5. See David Aran, 'Od kama he'arot al "Molcho" ('More Comments on "Molcho"'), *Al Hamishmar*, 5 June 1988.

6. For example, his son's name, Omri, is mentioned for the first time on p.29, his daughter's name, Anat, is mentioned for the first time on p.44,

the legal adviser's name, Miriam, on p. 107. The name of the cousin in Paris is not mentioned at all, nor is the name of the father of the young girl from Zeru'a. The name of Yair Ben-Yaish from the northern settlement is mentioned only later on in the story, and Molcho never addresses him by name.

7. In this respect, as in some others, Molcho is reminiscent of Yaakov Shabtai's novels *Zichron devarim (Past Continuous)* and *Sof davar (Past Perfect)*, but to analyse this analogy is beyond the scope of the present work.

8. *Ha'ir*, 20 March 1987, reported that Yehoshua decided to write about death in answer to a friend who had asked him after Shabtai's *Past Perfect* came out, 'How do people like this die?'. Dan Laor, op. cit., marvelled at Yehoshua's artistic achievement in representing the trauma of death, and suggested that the archetypal struggle of Eros and Thanatos is the source of the psychological and moral tensions underlying the book.

9. Abraham Hagorni-Green, 'Sipporet bat yameinu' ('Contemporary Hebrew Narrative'), *Or-Am*, 1989, p.51.

10. Susan Sontag, *Illness as Metaphor* (London: Allen Lane, 1978), pp.72–3.

11. Notice a similar use of rain in Ruth Almog's novel *Death in the Rain* (see Ch. 3).

12. See also pp.270, 297.

13. Yosef Oren, *Tziyonut vetzabariyut baroman ha-Yisra'eli (Zionism and Sabraism in the Israeli Novel)* (Rishon Letzion: Yahad, 1990), p.38.

14. Ortsion Bartana has suggested that this situation is reminiscent of the narrator's impossible love for an 11-year-old girl in the story *Atzabim (Nerves)* by Y. H. Brenner (Tel Aviv: Hakibbutz Hameuchad, 1956). See 'Zehirut, sifrut Eretz-Yisra'elit' (*Caution, Israeli Literature*), *Papyrus*, 1989, p.89.

15. He does not even know Vivaldi's *Four Seasons*, that popular classic.

16. In the context of Israeli society, Molcho's position in the army as a male nurse can be regarded as feminine. His preoccupation with domestic chores and with his weight, which causes the growth of small breasts (p.282), are some of the other obvious pointers.

17. See Doreet Hopp's interesting article, 'Molcho bashe'ol' ('Molcho in the Underworld'), *Siman Keri'ah*, Vol. 20 (May 1990), pp.473–79.

18. Shlomith Rimmon-Kenan, *Narrative Fiction: Contemporary Poetics* (London: Methuen, 1983), pp.69–70.

19. Here I disagree with the criticism that the structure of the novel lacks progression, voiced by Yehudit Oryan 'Lehamit be'ahava' ('To Kill with Love'), *Yediot Aharonot*, 6 Feb. 1987, and by Ortsion Bartana, 'Sipur marshim umefutzal' ('An Impressive and Diverse Story'), *Davar*, 6 March 1987.

20. On the importance of the Nibelungen in the story, see A. Balaban, *Mar Molcho (Mr Molcho)* (Tel Aviv: Hakibbutz Hameuchad, n.d.), pp.118–27.

21. Wolfgang Iser, *The Act of Reading: A Theory of Aesthetic Response* (London: Routledge & Kegan Paul, 1978), p.168.
22. Pp.96–102 and then pp.107–12 describe nothing but her condition.
23. See Michal Ne'eman, 'Ma nish'ar la'asot?' ('What is there left to do?'), *Yediot Aharonot*, 13 April1987.
24. Abraham Hagorni-Green, op. cit., p.53.
25. See his book review in *Davar*, op. cit.

3
Death in the Rain
by RUTH ALMOG

Death affects the course of the lives of all the characters in Almog's book and serves as one of the few threads to hold this fragmented story together. The narrator cum 'editor', Professor Licht, presents the story which he has pieced together from various documents written by the three other protagonists. Elisheva Green, a former student and lover of his, has sent him fragments of her diary[1] and the draft of a story which she wrote later, with random letters from one Alexander to his dying Greek friend Yanis, and Yanis's own unfinished written story. Elisheva has asked Licht to edit these documents and to reconstruct a story which would make sense. This is nearly an impossible task, as he testifies in the epilogue: 'Another matter which I must mention here is the great difficulty I had in constructing this book. From the outset I had to face the problem of building a rational construction from all these fragments, and indeed I had nothing more in my hands than fragments. I believe that I did all I could' (p. 198).[2]

This comment is one of many interspersing the story which draw the reader's attention to its metafictional character. This is self-conscious fictional writing, addressing an aesthetic challenge of art, that of discussing itself in its own language. The novel includes within itself a commentary on its own linguistic and narrative identity, constantly reminding the reader that fiction is an artefact.[3] Professor Licht discusses the process of writing. He finds structuring the book as confusing as sorting out a jigsaw puzzle (p.117). This, of course, is the voice of the author referring the reader to her novel, which is presented in a confused and fragmented form. Thus she instructs the reader to piece the fragments together, like the narrator of the novel, in order to be able to find some sense in the confused presentation of the story. She explicitly calls the reader's imaginative process

into action. Presumably concerned about the success of her chosen mode of writing, Almog adds an apologetic note. At times
too laboriously, she tries to explain that, whilst being fully
aware that the confused style of narration may deter the reader
from attaining a perfect picture, ultimately the actual creation,
the fiction, is what matters the most (p.117). However, because
of the author's preoccupation with the 'diegetic', or the narrative process, it becomes apparent that she does in fact want the
reader to be interested in how art is created, not just in what is
created. The four writers of the documents comment on the
aesthetic and emotional problems confronting a writer. From
this the reader is able to abstract and follow the author's
attempt to present a mimesis of the creative process, and of the
principles regarding writing in general and her own writing in
particular.

Elisheva would like to have written a story rather than a
diary. She believes that she is unable to do so because she is
unable to detach herself sufficiently from her own life to be
objective when describing it. However, she soon discovers that
even when writing a diary she has to create an artificial distance
between herself and her writing, so she cannot be entirely personal and spontaneous. She confesses:

> I am very pedantic about my style and I try to be accu-
> rate when writing. And so, a quality of writing
> emerges which is no longer typical of a diary. It is less
> spontaneous. To begin with I simply wrote. No defi-
> nite intentions. Now I am writing with the idea that
> one day this material will serve me as a basis for a
> firmer structure. I am conscious of the deception
> which is inherent in this kind of writing, of the pre-
> tence, of the selectivity. Passion is very strong, but so
> is fear. I chose the present tense and I relive events as
> I am writing them. And as I relive them it gives me the
> opportunity to interpret and shape them as I wish.
> (p.38)

She explains that her passion to shape characters, to imagine
events, to document facts, is related to her desire to leave some-

thing behind, even if it is only her words. She reflects that when she walks around the streets of Tel Aviv, she has the urge to write down everything her eyes can see; to write a book comprised of sights, a kind of 'map of words', or a 'verbal photograph' (p.16). This is certainly the author's voice explaining the drive behind the act of writing.

In retrospect Elisheva can see that writing is for her a narcissistic exercise, yet she feels that she has to do it for her self-preservation (p.52). Writing is therapeutic for her and through it she can compensate for the vitality which she misses in her real life (p.55). The therapeutic effect of writing is also experienced by the narrator. He is on the verge of a nervous breakdown when he receives the fragmented writings in the post: he decides to undertake the writing of his book. Through the act of writing he manages to rehabilitate himself and to sort out his own emotionally disturbed state.

Naively, Elisheva thinks that there is no difference between the two different literary genres of a diary and a narrative novel, since, she assumes, distance is required equally in both forms. Both serve as therapeutic and rehabilitating media. Corresponding to her protagonist, Almog herself uses both types of writing in *Death in the Rain*. Thus, indirectly, she warns readers that the two genres do require two different literary techniques and that they should not fall into the same trap as her protagonist initially does. Almog indirectly raises the important question of whether the reader should have a different or the same approach to the two different types of texts.

The third chapter of the novel is entitled 'The Visit to Carmella' and its epigraph contains a short biographical detail about the American poet Hart Crane. This chapter is Elisheva's attempt to abandon her diary and to write in what seems to her the more ambitious style of a 'story'. She is frustrated with the realisation that even in fiction she has to be true to life and to reflect her real tragedy, rather than invent a more palatable 'happy ending'. This is why she decides not to succumb to writing happy love stories, and to have the great novels such as *Jane Eyre* or *Wuthering Heights* as her model instead, all of which end tragically (p.132). So the content, as well as the form of her writing, concerns her. She knows that she cannot keep away from the subject of love and confesses that she would like to write love poetry but cannot (p.86). Yet soon after this proclamation about her inadequacy Elisheva goes on to write very romantically about her love. The narrator, unlike Elisheva, believes that love is unnecessary, and that its imprints are as insignificant as 'crumbs of happiness alongside immense suffering' (p. 198). He thinks that love is only fit for fiction, and that real life is better off without emotional involvement, which is always associated with suffering. Ironically, it is he who continually pursues love in his private life. The reader can detect the explanatory, almost apologetic, voice of the author about her preoccupation with the subject of love, and with raising the dilemma of its worth. After all, the quest for love of the three couples stands at the centre of Almog's novel.[4] It seems that they all like the idea of love more than the object of their love itself (p.92).

Elisheva has always wanted to become a real writer but she is afraid of failure. Lacking confidence, she sits in front of empty sheets of paper, unable to write anything. 'The story, which was formulated to the minutest detail in my head, would suddenly slip away, as if I was seized by paralysis' (p.52). Only when she is in Greece, away from the events she has described, can she manage to write a draft of her life story, based on her diary. Licht explains that he has decided not to alter the version which she has sent him, even though he regards it as merely an immature attempt at writing (p.71).

The narrator himself is also a frustrated writer, as are Yanis and Alexander. As a young science student in Oxford he wrote several short stories and published one, which was written, significantly, in English rather than in Hebrew. Surely he expresses here the frustration of most minority-language writers: 'It is such a lamentable waste to write for such a limited reading public' (p.61). Yanis also writes in English but, unlike the narrator, it is because he is 'a man without a language' (p.52). However, this is not quite true. Although Greek is his mother tongue, he always studies in English, and it is only since deciding to become a scientist that he has lost his linguistic interests altogether. So, the reason the two men do not become writers is not a lack of language, but the unbridgeable clash between art and science. Apparently different skills of expression are needed for these two genres. Licht notes: 'A scientist and a Romantic simply cannot go together' (p.197). He is told by the real and famous Kingsley Amis that he will never succeed in becoming a first-class writer, but that if he were to engage himself in non-fictional discourse, such as articles, research or journalism, he might succeed (p.52). Indeed, Professor Licht becomes a well-known scholar who publishes many academic papers. Once again Almog draws the reader's attention to the use of different literary genres. She begs us to analyse our responses to them and to examine whether or not they can all be genuinely treated in the same way. Almog's use of various genres within her novel forces the issue and emphasises the importance she attaches to this poetic question. It compels us as readers to examine our preconceived ideas about the novel.

The narrator-editor confides his intimate deliberations about writing his book to the reader. In one of many intervening editorial comments, he discloses that he initially intended to present the story as an objective account, without involving himself in it (see pp.70 and 145). After starting to write, however, he decides to incorporate his own life, which inevitably brings in sentimentality. The third writer, Yanis, is not prepared to compromise in this way. Having realised the importance of compromise in becoming a successful novelist, for many years he abandons writing in favour of science. Almog asks the reader, once again, to consider the differences between the arts and the sciences. Yanis starts to write a draft of his story only when he is dying and his time is running out, knowing that he will never complete it. In the event, the book which he so wants to write is found in the form of sporadic notes after his death (p.147). The reader's attention is again drawn to the fact that *Death in the Rain* itself is structured in the same sporadic fashion. The question which comes to mind is whether this form of writing can ever be regarded as 'something complete and all-embracing' (p.156). As mentioned earlier, this very question is raised by the narrator, and its importance is indicated by the fact that it is repeated, this time by Yanis.

Back in his homeland, Greece, Yanis regrets that he has put off writing, thus frustrating his creative drive (p.152). Even Elisheva regards him as a born poet, yet he himself doubts the extent of his originality. He often thinks in metaphors, but because he reads a great deal of poetry, Yanis is aware that he must be using other poets' metaphors, consciously or otherwise.[5] Almog raises major philosophical questions such as whether originality exists and, assuming that it does, where the fine line separating originality from plagiarism lies. She employs intertextuality, refering continually to other literary works and fictional characters. Elisheva's whole life, for example, is affected by Hart Crane's life and poetry, as well as by Tolstoy's Bazuchov in *War and Peace*, and others.[6] In using these devices of intertextuality and self-reference, Almog draws the reader's attention to the status of literature as an artefact, and poses questions about the relationship between fiction and reality. I would now like to draw out one thread from the fabric of the novel and turn to the role of 'place' in the book.

Place

The epigraph of the first chapter, which recurs in the narration itself (for example, on pp.7 and 23), already indicates that 'place' has an important function in the novel. It consists of two lines from a poem by the Hebrew poet Avraham Ben-Yitzhak: 'Happy are they that sow and shall not reap/ for they shall wander far away'.[7] It alludes to, and at the same time negates, the message contained in the Psalms (127:5) which says 'They that sow in tears shall reap in joy'. Whilst the Psalm refers to the joy of the Return to Zion and to the idea of permanent settlement and its material rewards, Ben-Yitzhak refutes the material aspect of this teaching. The poem suggests the opposite of the message of the Biblical verse, postulating that those without permanent attachments to a place are better off, because they are free to wander wherever they choose. The propagation of this idea is unexpected since it is directly opposed to the Zionist ideology of which Ben-Yitzhak was a spokesman. Here Almog uses another text, in this case the poem by Ben-Yitzhak, for the purpose of examining the implications of not adhering to the teachings of Zionism.

Licht traces the reasons for the unfulfilled Zionist dream back to the time that the Israelis lost physical contact with their land and started to wander away, either to an urban existence or, further away, to life abroad. He and his brother are examples of this latter trend: after the death of their father they sold his land and moved away. Licht's childhood home no longer exists. The Israel of small tiled houses and of farmers tilling the land and harvesting their olives has vanished (p.67). The father was a Second Aliyah pioneer who, like many of his contemporaries, fulfilled his socialist ideology by working the land with his own hands. Licht believes that in those early days of Zionism peoples' lives were worthier than now because working the land was central to their chosen way of life. In contemporary Israel land no longer has the practical purpose that it used to have (p.67). People have started to use land as an ornament, as a demonstration of their social class and material achievements. He mourns the loss of the simple, unsophisticated life, as well as the advent of modernity. Above all, Licht blames the Israelis, himself included, for distancing themselves from their own landscape:

> People live in big cities and they suffocate. On the festival days they go to the forests and have picnics, bringing charcoal grills and spits for roasting with. They only sense the landscape through the smoke rising from their camp-fires. As they return home they leave litter behind them. One should not really be surprised by what happens when people lose their real contact with the land. They are corrupted. (p.25)

Gershon Shaked has noted that Israeli literature of the 1980s wishes to restore the lost paradise rather than find a new one.

> The past is presented as the opposite of the present: the founding fathers are magnificant human beings; the sons are mere grasshoppers; the land of orchards opposes the world of contractors . . . pioneering Israel

stands out against the country that has indentured itself to various golden calves . . . utopia is the reality of the past; the present is nothing but a great and ugly dystopia.[8]

Licht and his brother reject their father's way of life. They do not fulfil the Psalm's verse, 'They that sow in tears shall reap in joy', but choose to wander. His brother leaves for the comfort of material life in America, and he himself for the comfort of academic life in renowned international seats of learning such as Oxford, Harvard and, later, those in Israel. Their father met with opposition and disappointment not only from his children but also from his own contemporaries. Unlike the richer Jewish landowners of the First Aliyah, he followed the principles of Zionism and worked the land himself, resisting the employment of cheap Arab labour. He also insisted on speaking Hebrew at home rather than French, even though French was regarded as a more aristocratic language at that time, more suitable for intellectual and cultural conversations. He refused to use any other language associated with the way of life he had left behind. The irony is that Licht strives to recapture the European identity which his father sacrificed for the sake of his beliefs. Licht is ashamed of the coarseness of the Sabra's behaviour and mannerisms, which he tries hard to refine in himself. It is no coincidence that he becomes an art historian, specialising in European art. It may also be no coincidence that his wife is the daughter of an established landowner, speaks French and is at home with European culture. Licht reflects that, ironically, it was she who found it hard to adapt to life abroad and dreamt of their return: 'She was not happy anywhere. Transience frightened her. Only here, in this flat, where we settled down after she persuaded me to return to Israel, was she happy' (p.8).

Thus, through Licht, Almog voices a severe criticism of life in Israel today, as well as that of the past. Licht only describes the place when comparing it with the past. He never describes it per se. So, for example, when he finds himself in a small corner of Tel Aviv looking at the ugly modern buildings around him, he cannot help reflecting nostalgically that they have been built in a place where a much nicer quiet street, with modest low-roofed houses, once existed (p.5).

Elisheva also reflects nostalgically on the lost places of her childhood, when utopia had been made real for her. She is very upset to see that the charming old houses of early Tel Aviv have been neglected and turned into offices and agencies of all kinds (p.32). She regards buildings as an expression of people's culture and ideals, and is ashamed of these. In contrast with Haifa, Tel Aviv is appalling in its bestial ugliness:

> Monster's jaws gaped at me; the black cavities of the staircases, shattered windows, looking like memorials of the Holocaust on these sooty buildings. Their fronts are delapidating, and the balconies, with their peeling plaster, expose rusty iron bars. An overt, shameless strip-tease. On the balconies there are folksy latticed iron railings, a remnant of some charm, of some insistence on aestheticism. Now they are twisted, rusty and half-torn. In the midday sun of the wintery warmth, the hard light emphasises the ugliness. (pp.12–13; further examples on pp.33, 72, 74)

The city and its trees are slowly consumed by soot and dust, except for a brief time during early spring, when the blossom purifies the air. In some forgotten corners of Tel Aviv one can still discover wild flowers growing in the rubble as reminders of better days.

It seems that the only positive aspects of Elisheva's contemporary environment are those which have been untouched by modernity. In a masterful description of another corner of Tel Aviv – where there are mainly food wholesalers' shops and small eating-places, with many people of oriental origin speaking 'a different Hebrew and sometimes Ladino' (p.57) – Almog most sensitively captures the smells and flavours of the food associated with this place. Elisheva finds that one can really get to know people's tastes, desires and delights. It is probably because it has remained unchanged, untouched by the sophistication of modern city life, that she is drawn to it. 'There was

something marvellously picturesque in this tumult, some wonderful vitality' (p.56). Excepting this corner, Elisheva deplores
Tel Aviv as it is now: like Licht, she sets it against the lost paradise of her childhood. She too mourns the unfulfilled Zionist
dream that has become a disappointment. Licht portrays the
social and intellectual changes which have taken place, and
Elisheva portrays the aesthetic changes. Both come to the conclusion that the race for material achievements is one of the
most deplorable changes in contemporary Israel. Elisheva, for
example, sarcastically observes the Israelis' absurd craze for the
latest and most fashionable household gadgets, all to impress
their friends (p.16). Her chosen profession is landscape archi-
tecture and she views her surroundings through this prism.
(This interest in the external environment may be the result of
trying to escape from delving into her own internal world.)

Although Alexander is mentally ill, it is he who voices a view
of place that sounds saner than that of the others. He is satisfied
with life in Tel Aviv and cannot understand why the Israelis
'always complain about this country and its lack of culture'
(p.20). Those aspects of life in the city which prove negative for
Licht and Elisheva are positive for him. The crowded
pavements offer him comfort, and the people sitting idly in
coffee houses, companionship. It does not bother him, for
example, that the mental home in which he spends most of his
time once belonged to a rich Arab. It seems that Alexander has
reached this complacent attitude through bitter disappoin-
ments. His colleagues' conventional, academic approach to
science suffocated his flare for experimentation and drove him
far away, to a kibbutz in the desert. Yanis, his best friend,
suggests that this move was his way of escaping from a culture
and civilisation which limited and rejected him. It was a kind of
a self-imposed exile (p.161). The unique qualities which
attracted Alexander to the desert are the antithesis of those of
the city:

> God placed large stones there with irregularity, and
> broken granite slabs, smooth, white, and shining in
> the sun like marble. Large, white bones of different
> animals could be seen in the openings of the caves in

71

the red sandy stone. . . . At night we heard the wail-
ing of the wind, the call of the night birds seeking
their prey; cries of wandering stray camels, or was it
that of a caravan of camels, secretly making its way
from border to border? (p. 161)

The only thing which now concerns Alexander about his environment is that the Israelis choose to ape European aesthetic
tastes, without adapting them to the requirements of their landscape. When he looks around him in the municipal park in Tel
Aviv, he thinks it ridiculous that the lawns and bushes are
trimmed in exactly the same fashion as they are in England:
'land is too costly, and apart from that, this does not suit its
nature at all' (p.136). Alexander's obsession with making
Chinese paper-gardens provides him with the pretext to escape
from his immediate surroundings, and allows him the freedom
to express his aesthetic creativity. Thus, unlike Elisheva and
Licht, he is able to accommodate his disappointments with life,
although in a peculiar way, and to come to terms with his environment. His lone voice counterbalances the view presented by
the other two Israeli characters in the novel, and forces the
reader to decide whether one should be satisfied with or critical of life in Israel.

The novel voices criticism of life in Israel in the wake of disappointment with the unfulfilled Zionist dream. It exposes the
negative aspects of contemporary life by deploring the constant
race for material achievements, which has replaced ideology. It
reveals the unaesthetic manifestations of urbanised life and crit-
icises the social, intellectual and environmental changes which
have affected the place. However, what is of particular interest
here is that one of the poetic devices by which the author
expresses this criticism is the use of place.

Although the tension between home and abroad is not central in this novel, it is nevertheless present throughout.
Alexander continually compares life in Greece with life in
Israel. Yet he is not blinded by the appearance of Greece and
mocks his friend Yanis, whose view is always tainted by a
romantic idealisation of life. Alexander could never love a place
as passionately. He is sceptical about the apparent good life of

the Greeks which he has seen, or imagines to have seen, with Yanis: 'I saw the wet washing dripping water from one wall to the next, piles of wooden and metal tubs, shrubs of herbs planted in clay pots, people doing their work, and I asked myself if these women, labouring over the buckets of washing, really longed for washing machines' (p.120). Alexander concludes that they did, and therefore assumes that life is the same wherever one is. Escaping to another country cannot solve personal problems of any sort.

Elisheva holds the opposite view. After the terrible disappointment over her love affair with Licht and the loss of their illegitimate baby, she seeks comfort abroad and joins her friend Yanis in Italy, where he in turn is trying to recover from the loss of Henrietta. They hope to find comfort in one another, as well as in the foreign environment, but to no avail. To both of them, Venice and its decaying beauty are oppressive, and they are bored. Their sinking relationship is reflected in the sinking city. The reader brings the romantic associations of Venice to the text and is surprised to discover that this place does not charm the two protagonists: 'We climbed one of the bridges and leant on the railings, looking at the filthy black water. A black gondola passed by. It was a clear morning and tourists sat in the gondola. A young Italian boy sang a familiar Italian song for them in a high clear voice' (p. 44). When Yanis sees the gondola all he can think about is how fitting this setting would have been for the burial of his dead Henrietta. Thus, thoughts of death pursue the characters, even in a place such as Venice. The change of location does not change their feelings. On the contrary, the descriptions of the different places emphasise the unchangeability of their emotions.

Escaping to a place where she does not belong and to which she feels no obligations is Elisheva's wish: 'I must go away from here, to a far away place where I don't know anyone, to a distant corner of the world where a primeval silence prevails, the quietness of the beginning of the world, the tranquillity of death of a distant time' (p.86). She is attracted to Greece because of what it stands for, not necessarily by the place itself. For her this is a place where the landscape has made an eternal pact with God to remain unchanged, unlike modern Israel. Even when she imagines her forthcoming visit to Greece she thinks of it in terms of ancient olive trees and temples. Using Biblical language and imagery, she conjures a description of Greece where farmers are still tilling the earth themselves, returning home in the evenings carrying wooden ploughs on their backs (p.87). The comparison to the early days of Zionism and the contrast with life in Israel today are evident. The place stands as a metonym, and through its descriptions Elisheva voices her criticism of life in Israel. Yanis claims that Elisheva is restless, not so much because of her need to run away, but because she and her fellow Israelis do not have earthly ties with their land. They have no anchor. To Yanis, the Greeks love their land through the earthly passions of food and wine, whilst the Israelis love their land through suffering. In this respect, as Yanis thinks, the Israelis are the ones to have inherited the teachings of Jesus, so it is ironic that Elisheva is the one to echo the Christian idea of yearning to make ties with life through death and suffering (p.77).

This reversal of historical roles, and the meeting of two extremes, brings to mind Derrida's argument regarding double identity and the Other: 'Are we Jews? Are we Greeks? We live in the difference between the Jew and the Greek, which is perhaps the unity of what is called history.'[9] According to this argument, it is essential to think through the synthesis of Greek and Jew. Furthermore, as Susan Handelman has pointed out, Derrida regards the Greek/Jew synthesis as being parallel to the poet/rabbi conflict: 'The conflict is identified as heteronomy versus autonomy, the poet's freedom versus the rabbi's subjection to Law . . . one interpretation nostalgically seeking origin, the other affirming free play . . . the two interpretations, though irreconcilable, are lived simultaneously – and there is no possibility of choosing between them.' [10] The Greek philosophical tradition in the West has the Jew as 'the Other' and this enables double identity to exist, which is what Almog is exploring.

The earthly passions of the Greeks are central in the fifth and last chapter of the novel, indicatively entitled 'The Bread'. It is singled out by being the only chapter which is not preceded

by an epigraph and it consists of the outlines for a book written
by the dying Yanis, in Greece. Following preliminary references
to Greece earlier in the story, the scene finally shifts to Greece,
and ultimately to the direct comparison between Israel and
Greece, between home and abroad. The comparison, which had
focused on the differences between the two, now elicits the similarities. It is based on observations of people, ideology and history: Yanis, like many of his Israeli friends, returns to his
homeland after a long exile. His country was ruled for many
years by the Turks, as was Israel, before it gained its independence. His father and many of his father's contemporaries
believed in socialism, as did the early Zionists. Furthermore,
both nations have common characteristics such as their restlessness and their love of commerce. These are somewhat superfi-
cial comparisons, but they enable the author to introduce the
idea of one single Mediterranean culture, bound by common
characteristics and a common history within the same geographical area.

The reader is fully aware that there is no such pluralistic concept as 'Mediterranean culture', and that there are hundreds of
cultures, languages, dialects and literatures in this region. But,
as Yoram Bronowsky has suggested, the theory of one single and
all-embracing culture does exist.[11] This is a humanistic idea
modelled on the culture of the Hellenistic period; in *Death in
the Rain*, it is through Yanis, the Greek character who lives most
of his life in Israel, that it finds expression. Almog suggests that
young yet complex cultures, such as those of modern Israel or
modern Greece, need to adopt such an idea. It could be a meeting point of strangers and suggests the possibility of friendly co-
existence that is so important for both places, thereby
extending its scope to the Arabs in Israel. A. B. Yehoshua claims
that an Israeli identity should be considered in terms of its
Mediterranean, rather than Near Eastern, context:

> I think that 'Mediterranean' is a key word in under-
> standing and talking about Israel. In the early days, peo-
> ple argued the question whether Israel would be western
> or oriental. Some of us realized that Israel would have to
> integrate into the region. Our region is not the [Near]

East so much as it is a region of the Mediterranean. It is
Greece and Italy and Egypt and Malta and Turkey. That
is our true environment. We don't have to visualize our-
selves in the context of Iraq or Iran or Saudi Arabia.
They are not our true neighbors.[12]

It is clear that the descriptions of Greece here function
metaphorically. However, I would like to point out that it is a
special kind of metaphor which is employed. It does not simply
designate the context from which it emerges, but it is generated
by metonymic transfer, and thus allows us to speak of Greece as
a metaphor supported by metonymy.

Stephen Ullman has distinguished between these two types
of imagery, suggesting that the metaphorical is based on a relationship of similarity whilst the metonymic is based on an external relationship of contiguity.[13] Although Roman Jakobson has
claimed that 'these two tropes are in a relationship of competi-
tion such that one or the other will prevail in a given discourse',
I would like to pursue the line of argument of Gérard Genette,
who has proposed that 'metaphor and metonymy support each
other and interpenetrate one another . . . showing the presence
and action of relations of "coexistence" at the very heart of the
relation of analogy'.[14] The link in Almog's novel between
Greece and Israel is based not so much on some hidden resemblance or analogy, but rather on an external relation: both happen to be Mediterranean and as a result assume similarities.
This accidental relationship is brought about by juxtaposition,
rather than by relying on essential resemblance: thus Greece is
presented as metonymic rather than metaphorical. Metonymy
requires a context for its operation and this is why Jakobson
links it with realism: 'Realism speaks of its object by offering
the reader aspects, parts, and contextual details, in order to
evoke a whole.'[15] The similar features of Greece and Israel are
the two parts which create the context, and their identity is
asserted through metonymy. David Lodge has noted that 'the
metaphor-metonymy distinction is a powerful tool for analysing
and categorizing literary discourse. . . . it may be that the tension or "dialogue" between them is one of the most significant
features of a text.'[16]

76

Places in Israel, on the other hand, are metaphorical. John Searle has suggested that 'the basic principle on which all metaphor works is that the utterance of an expression with its literal meaning and corresponding truth conditions can, in various ways that are specific to metaphor, call to mind another meaning and corresponding set of truth conditions.'[17] Elisheva regards place as being the cultural expression of ideas, and thus creates the link between those ideas and place. There is an essential resemblance between a particular place (here, Tel Aviv) and that which it represents. As we have seen, contemporary Tel Aviv is described in negative terms only, and these correspond to the negative terms in which contemporary Zionist ideology is presented. Contrasting with the ugliness of the city, stands the beauty of the early settlements, which in turn corresponds to the beautiful ideology held by the early settlers. Both types of places, those of today and those of the past, and both Israel and Greece, represent in metaphor or metonym their own essential qualities. They are used as poetic tools for structuring a metaphor or a metonym that represents ideological thinking.

NOTES

1. The fragments appear in the following order: 12 Feb. 1969, 18 Feb. 1969, 19 Feb. 1969; four short notes from March 1969; three short notes from 1957; and a tiny scrap from 1963. (It seems to me that the inclusion of the fragments from 1957 just burdens the reader with an excessive number of fragments, without adding anything to the text.) English translation by Dalya Bilu, *Death in the Rain* (Santa Fe, New Mexico: Red Crane Books, 1993).
2. For the purpose of this analysis all translations are my own.
3. See Patricia Waugh, *Metafiction* (London: Methuen, 1984).
4. The unfulfilled loves are that of Alexander for Henrietta (Elisheva's best friend at primary school; clever, beautiful yet an introvert; arrived in Israel in her early teens as an orphan and Holocaust survivor); Yanis for Henrietta; Elisheva for Licht.
5. As, for example, likening his life to 'the black bread of the peasants' (p.150).
6. A wide range of works are mentioned: see pp.33, 50, 54, 90, 117, 142, 147, 154 and many more.
7. His surname was Sone; he was born in Galicia in 1883 and died in Israel

in 1950. Although he did not write that many poems in Hebrew, he was one of the first to introduce Modernism to Hebrew poetry.

8. Gershon Shaked, 'Challenges And Question Marks: On the Political Meaning of Hebrew Fiction in the Seventies and Eighties', *P.E.N. Israel, 1991, A Collection of Recent Writing in Israel* (Ramat Gan: Institute for the Translation of Hebrew Literature, 1991), p.110.

9. Jacques Derrida, 'Structure, Sign, and Play' (1966), cited by Susan Handelman, 'Parodic Play and Prophetic Reason: Two Interpretations of Interpretation', *Poetics Today* (Durham, NC: Duke University Press), Vol. 9, No. 2 (1988), p.400.

10. Op. cit., pp.400–1.

11. Yoram Bronowsky, 'Yam tichoniyut, eich?' ('Mediterranean, How?'), *Ha-Aretz*, 12 Oct. 1990.

12. Cited in Joseph Cohen, *Voices of Israel* (State University of New York Press, 1990), p.71. See also the Introduction, p.15, n. 19, this volume.

13. Cited by Jonathan Culler, *The Pursuit of Signs* (London: Routledge & Kegan Paul, 1983), p.189.

14. Cited by Jonathan Culler, op. cit., pp.192–3.

15. Cited by Raman Selden, *Reader's Guide to Contemporary Literary Theory* (London: Harvester Press, 1988), p.64.

16. David Lodge, *After Bakhtin: Essays on Fiction and Criticism* (London: Routledge, 1990), p.6.

17. John Searle, 'Metaphor', in Andrew Ortony (ed.), *Metaphor and Thought* (Cambridge University Press, 1981), p.99.

4

Minotaur

by BENJAMIN TAMMUZ

Minotaur alludes to two different sources, one visual and one
literary. The first source is an etching made by Picasso in 1933,
a reproduction of which is printed on the front cover of
Tammuz's book, and the second is the classical story from
Greek mythology. These allusions must obviously have a bearing on the novel's interpretation. Picasso's etching, entitled
Dying Minotaur in Arena, shows a young girl stretching her
hand in a desperate attempt to touch and comfort a dying monster, half man and half bull. However, it is quite clear from the
picture that her hand will not reach the minotaur before it dies.
The etching is one of a sequence of mythological monsters, all
of which are seen as grotesque amalgams of a female griffin and
a minotaur. The theme of the minotaur is presented by Picasso
in various ways,[1] and can be seen in the context of the Surrealist
movement's search for new symbols to express the ills of the
1930s. The Surrealists found the minotaur a suitable symbol for
human bestiality and the violence of the modern age. It has
been pointed out that 'Picasso amended the symbolism; as if to
say that the brutishness of human society was as mindless as the
forces of nature, he made the minotaur innocent in his destruc-
tiveness'.[2] In his engravings it appears both menacing and harm-
less, a tender seducer and a lecherous creature. Despite the
minotaur's overwhelming power, his muscular body and his
menacing horns, his eyes often have a gentle look, stressing the
human part of the creature.[3]

Minotauros, the monster of Greek mythology and the source
of the Surrealists' inspiration, is also half man and half bull. It
was the offspring of the wife of Minos, the ruler of Crete, and
the white bull sent to him by the god Poseidon for sacrifice. As
a punishment for not sacrificing the bull, Minos's wife was

made to fall in love with it, and gave birth to the monster, which was shut up in a specially built labyrinth.[4] This tale echoes the story of the minotaur's ancestors. Its grandfather, the god Zeus, disguised himself as a white bull, abducted Europa (the mortal beautiful daughter of the king of Phoenicia) and carried her away to a cave on the island of Crete. Myth, which is a story that symbolises deep-lying aspects of human existence,[5] has been much used in contemporary fiction. Tammuz draws on several themes from the minotaur myth to create his own version of the story.

Both Picasso's engraving and the Greek tale have many similarities with the novel. All three are stories of unattainable love. The narrator in our novel is a secret agent who, on his forty-first birthday, falls in love with Thea, a beautiful young girl, 24 years his junior, a stranger, who is not even aware of his existence. His love for her is reminiscent of Zeus's love for Europa, and warns of a similarly unhappy ending as that of the Greek myth. The framework for an analogical interpretation of the novel is thus created.

The story is divided into four chapters, each subdivided into several short sections. The first chapter is entitled 'Secret Agent' and the others bear names of people. The story unfolds through a third-person narration, a diary and a series of letters, making the narrative inconsistent and unstable. In this novel, as in Tammuz's trilogy,[6] the prevailing form is satire, with its parodic and grotesque elements.[7] The linguistic register of the narration is not higher than functional, and the dialogues are banal, invariably spoofs. At times they read like a translation, to create the effect of the characters speaking in some language other than Hebrew (p.45). The first chapter is the 'exposition' which, true to its function, contains all the characters and events of the story. Information about them is presented only partially, to reappear afterwards in different parts of the text. The reader, like a secret agent, has to collate the scattered information to piece the story together. In the style of a detective story, hints which are given in early parts of the novel come up again in slightly different versions or with additional details. The overlapping information, at times repeated verbatim, forces readers to check the variants, question them, and draw their own conclusions.[8]

Using his professional skills, the anonymous secret agent, who has a wife and three children somewhere unspecified, hires people to find out information about the young girl, Thea, whom he sees by chance. Having obtained it, he starts sending her some 400 unsigned letters over a period of nearly ten years. In these letters, written in a colloquial and banal style, he expresses his love for her and manages to arouse her curiosity and eventual love for him. Although Thea thinks he is cruel not to allow her to meet him, she accepts this bizarre relationship. He follows her progress through school, on to her graduation from university, and on to a small southern university where she teaches Spanish literature. During this period Thea becomes engaged to G. R. (the initials are never expanded), the son of upper-class neighbours of her parents, who, unbeknown to her, falls in love with her when they are still schoolchildren. Shortly before their wedding he is killed in an obscure car accident. Subsequently Thea gets involved with a visiting scholar from a Spanish university who, just like G. R. and the secret agent before him, falls in love with her at first sight. For her part, Thea is attracted to him only because he looks just like the photograph she has of the secret agent. The identification of the two men, albeit mistaken, calls for a comparison between them. This analogy is reinforced when the reader discovers both men's obsession with music, Mozart's in particular (pp. 24, 106). The secret agent finds it necessary to communicate with Thea not only through letters but also through records of Mozart's music, which he sends her regularly. The scholar's commitment to music is as deep, the reader learns later. He manages to resist his domineering father's pressure to stop playing the piano, and pursues his passion for it.

Thea, anxious to establish the identity of the Spanish visitor, insists on him telling his life story. She finds that he was born in Alexandria to rich Greek parents, who moved to the Lebanon. The reader, who by now is conditioned to treat with care any additional information, is alerted: the story is narrated in Hebrew and therefore it seems fair to assume that it should have some connection either with Israel or with Israelis. Since the location of the story has now moved to the Middle East, it is just possible that there is a connection between the scholar and the anonymous letter-writer who, perhaps, may be an Israeli. During the scholar's short stay with Thea and her parents, two shots are heard from the direction of the coffee house opposite, the same coffee house whence the secret agent had hired the old waiter to spy on her when he first saw her. Thea becomes alarmed, since in addition to the association with the place, she associates the shooting with the two shots about which the secret agent had written to her, aimed at him in Madrid some while beforehand. That event, he wrote, resulted in the disfiguration of his face and plastic surgery. Filled with fear that it is he who has been shot, she collapses. She is shown to be a very nervous person. When she first meets the scholar she has to take tranquillisers to calm her nerves, and it comes as no surprise that after the shooting incident a doctor has to be summoned. After she recovers, she goes to the chemist for some pills, where the pharmacist quotes from Shakespeare's Romeo and Juliet ('my poverty but not my will consents'), anticipating a tragic ending for the lovers of our novel.

The second chapter shifts to tell the story of G. R., whose father left home when the boy was 12, destroying the apparently happy and comfortable family life. The mother has a breakdown, after which she is no longer the same person. G. R.'s relationship with his mother takes an unexpected twist after he happens to see her naked. His incestuous sexual desires are aroused and when he falls in love with Thea he confuses the two women in his dreams. G. R. is sent to a prestigious boarding school where, not unexpectedly, he has a homosexual relationship with a boy in his dormitory. However, after watching Thea for three years from his bedroom window at home, G. R. introduces himself to her and eventually persuades her to become engaged to him. After university G. R. is rewarded for his achievement by his father, who gives him an expensive Lamborghini. He is all set to embark on a successful career in a business which his father has planned for him.

By the end of the next chapter the analogous structure on which the story hangs becomes complex. G. R. and the scholar are compared: their fathers are both successful businessmen and both expect their sons to follow in their footsteps. The theme of fathers and sons is one of the most important in the novel. In the Greek myth, the son, the minotaur, was punished for his forefather's sin of abducting his beloved (Europa) from her family. Similarly, in the Biblical version, the son is taken to be sacrificed for his father's beliefs. Tammuz condemns the fathers, as the secret agent himself confesses in the last chapter: 'I am the madman, and behind the upholstered and luxurious madness there lurks a father who allows his son to be dragged away and bound up ready for sacrifice' (p.185, English edition).⁹ Another analogy is created in the fourth chapter between G. R.'s boarding school and that of the secret agent's. Whilst the former strove for social elitism, the second strove for egalitarianism. There are many other parallels between G. R.'s story and that of the secret agent's. Both fall for Thea's looks at first sight, noticing particularly the black velvet ribbon tying her hair. Both meet and see her within the same year, and both develop their relationship with her through correspondence. Most significantly, both sit at the same coffee house where their fates are finally determined.

The third chapter shifts the focus to Nikos Trianda, the hitherto unnamed scholar. His story is repeated, but with additional information. When his parents moved from the Lebanon to Paris, he left home, joined his sister who was a singer in Berlin, changed his name, and eventually moved to Spain. Whilst in Germany he feels alienated from the northern part of Europe and longs for the places of his childhood. Not surprisingly, whilst in Germany he studies Greek at university, tracing the historical, cultural and linguistic roots of his ancestral background. He publishes in Paris a short volume of his research on the reawakening of the peoples of the Mediterranean, but the idea is received with criticism: 'in their eyes he was a Latin romantic, a southerner, with impaired powers of analysis and an excess of saccharine Eastern sentimentality' (p.96, English edition). The plot shifts to Israel. As part of his interest in pursuing the common features of the various Mediterranean cultures, Nikos travels around the region and arrives in Israel. Whilst staying there with one of his mother's relations, he is taken by the Israeli secret service to be interrogated about the relation's anti-Zionist activities. The reader is again alerted to connect the interrogator with Thea's anonymous lover. The possibility of his connection with Israel is reinforced.

On the surface level of the text, Nikos's interest in his roots and in Greece's glorious past evokes Greek mythology, and particularly the myth of the minotaur. His move to Spain evokes the name of Picasso, the Spanish painter of the minotaur. Thus, Nikos embodies the two different sources of the minotaur, the literary and the visual, both of which stand in the centre of this new version of the minotaur story. Thea's life too is linked to this dominant theme: she chooses to study Spanish and her thesis is about Luis de Gongora (1561–1627), one of the most influential Baroque Spanish poets. At one point she is even prepared to confess to Nikos that she has the blood of Spanish Jews on her father's side (p.73). Whilst her connections with Spain may provoke allusions to bulls and bullfighting and thus to Picasso – who stands for the visual dimension of the minotaur myth – the fact that she studies Spanish literature may be taken as a literary reference to the same myth. Tammuz himself practised a visual art also: he was a talented and prolific sculptor as well as a writer, so his use of visual dimensions of literature is another form of self-reference in the text.[10]

Only in the fourth chapter of the novel does it transpire that the secret agent of the first chapter is the Alexander Abramov, an Israeli, of this chapter. His father's name appears in different variations, deliberately confusing the reader.[11] This conventional strategy of a detective story forces the reader to try to fit the different pieces of the puzzle, to reconstruct a coherent picture. The two names are direct references to the Biblical patriarch who was prepared to sacrifice his son for his beliefs, on the one hand, and to the great Greek conqueror, on the other (his first name is Greek, like Nikos's, another similarity between the two men). The father was born in Russia, moved to France, then to Germany, and finally, disillusioned with the West, to Palestine in 1921. His movements from one place to another are analogous to the movement of locations of Nikos's father, during the same time in history and in the same region. At the age of 60 Alexander Abramov's father arrives in a southern Jewish settlement with his much younger German pregnant wife, and builds a large house on a huge estate which he has bought. The age gap between the parents is analogous to the gap between their son Alexander and Thea. Neither couple can reach happiness together. The family lives at a much higher standard than any of their neighbours, and leads an insular existence, at the centre of which stands music. The father took his Gentile wife away from her home to another continent, and just like his counterpart in the minotaur myth, is punished for it. At Alexander's birth, the mother's mental and emotional state become unstable and eventually, at the age of 36, she loses her mind. Music and the minotaur myth are specifically linked in a passage (p.126, English edition) that describes Alexander as a young boy going to sleep to the sound of his parents and their friends making music while he looks at the Picasso minotaur etching. He imagines three circles of music that listeners can penetrate and realises that no one can reach the third innermost circle of music (and life, Tammuz means the reader to understand) except when they die.

Alexander goes to the local school but is unable to mix with anyone, with the exception of Leah, the girl who sits next to him in class. Unexpectedly, the major event which determines the course of his life is not associated with his strange childhood, but with the murder of Leah's father during the 1929 Arab riots. On Alexander's Bar Mitzvah, which is marked by the family merely by a festive meal, he decides that when he grows up he will marry Leah and avenge her father's death. The decision to kill Arabs stands in stark contrast with the civilised, highly European cultural upbringing which he has at home. His choice of books reflects his obsessional streak and single-mindedness: he reads only about music, love and revenge, the three main desires which shape his life. Alexander is sent to an agricultural boarding school, where for the first time in his life he has no option but to mix with other pupils. However, the social, ideological and cultural differences between them are too wide to bridge, and he shuts himself away to be left with his records, his cello and his diary. During the first summer vacation, when he cannot go home because of his mother's poor health, he experiences both sex and revenge: he has sex with a married woman, which he knows is a betrayal, and he encounters a bedouin who threatens to kill him (p. 150, English edition). Alexander strangles the Arab to death, feeling that in so doing he is at last avenging the death of Leah's father. However, the image of the murdered bedouin haunts him for the rest of his life, accounting for his ambivalent attitude to the Arabs when he deals with them as a secret agent. He writes about this issue in his diary:

> These Arabs that I, in fact, persecute because they have fallen into my hands, handcuffed and beaten, who are they if not those same Arab labourers in the yards of our house; those same Arabs with whom I chased hares; those same Arabs whose working mothers would catch me secretly in the shed and cover my face with kisses. . . . Now I sit their sons down facing an electric light and repay them with mortal fears in return for the childhood joys I knew with them and for their mothers' love. I'm not apologizing. They regard us with deadly hatred and I'm just doing what is possible and necessary to do. But this does not alter the fact that in return for the friendship of one Arab I would give ten American, English, or French friends. With a European I can drink whiskey, do business, and come to an understanding that the state of Israel is in fact an extension of Europe in the east; but with an Arab I can once again roll about in the clods of the earth in the plantation, inhale the smell of an oven burning goat dung, pick and eat thyme, run toward the horizon and find my childhood there. (pp.183–4, English edition)[12]

Together with his friends at school he joins the Defence underground (the Haganah) and decides to become a professional soldier. His mother commits suicide – just as Thea does later on – his father dies, and he marries Leah. Alexander does try to leave the army and settle down to domestic life, but is unable to do so. He cannot be tied down to one place and lead a conventional life, so he joins the secret service. The report recommending him for the job sums up his character:

> He is a quintessential romantic vis-à-vis concepts of integrity, honour, and loyalty, but as a counterbalance to romanticism he has a well-developed sense of reality and astuteness. This does not make life easier for him, but makes him eminently suitable and extremely well qualified for intelligence duties and for missions demanding devotion, secrecy, and daring. (p.176, English edition)

It does not come as a complete surprise to discover that he was indeed the one who interrogated Nikos when he visited Israel. Thus, two different strands of the fabric of the story are drawn together. The end of the novel is the culmination of other strands which have been presented in different variations and which cause the reader to feel destabilised. Confirmation is given of the earlier open hints that the stranger who approached G. R. for the test-drive which causes his fatal accident is indeed Alexander, using the same name to approach Nikos at Thea's university. Another discovery which Alexander conceals from Thea is that he was put in prison when he produced the wrong passport on his way to her. It appears that he was exposed during his attempt to reach her, and the mutated story of Romeo and Juliet reaches its final scene when he is shot and she commits suicide.

Thea is as close to meeting Alexander as the young girl of Picasso's etching is to the minotaur. However, neither of the couples is destined to be united. Thea is his dream and Alexander is an image made up of words and of time. Ironically, finding Thea is not a find but a terrible loss, 'a loss which was discovered when all was lost' (p.16). Yosef Oren has pointed out that Tammuz's characters always suffer and are always in pain. Only through pain are they able to keep their own image and their desire for life. Most characters long to elevate themselves and reach for something spiritual, something which is

> the divine source of the soul. . . . through these long-
> ings the author expresses his humanistic and religious
> values. This is why he pours equal measure of love on
> the characters who were privileged to reach the object
> of their longings, and on those who did not. A human
> being's test is not success, but the longings, . . . for
> longings testify to humanity.[13]

However, reality can never match up with longing to attain per-
fection, and therefore, 'all places in the world are the same
place', as one of Tammuz's short stories' characters suggests.[14]
According to him, longings make everyone restless and in perpetual exile even when not aware of it. This is a situation like
that of the 'secular pilgrim', as noted in the Introduction.[15]

Nikos compares his dream of the reawakening of the
Mediterranean peoples to Alexander's and Thea's dreams of
love. Both represent the nonfulfilment of dreams, and as such
they resemble music. Music, which is so important in
Alexander's life, is always perceived by him in terms of three
circles one inside the other, as we have seen and as he notes in
his diary:

> Lately I have thought a lot about the three circles in
> music. I can pierce the first circle the moment I read
> the notes, hum a bit to myself, or try something out
> on the piano. I get the idea and I am already inside the
> first circle. I pierce the second circle when I listen
> closely to the music or when I play it more or less cor-
> rectly. Now comes the third circle. For what is music,
> in fact? It's speech. But the composer speaks not in
> words but in symbols. . . . If the listener has the
> strength and intelligence to pierce through to the cen-
> tre of music, that's a sign that the listener resembles
> the artist himself to some extent. (pp.148–9, English
> edition)

After seeing Thea, Alexander immediately knows that she is the
fulfilment of his dreams, awaiting him inside the third circle of

life. She is the figment of his imagination, an image which reveals itself wherever he is, be it Berlin, Zurich or Munich. He believes that he is ready to embark on a journey which will unite them – the journey of death – but, just like Picasso's minotaur, he is not united with Thea before he dies. The concept of the three circles, whether in dreams or in music, assumes a metaphoric function which extends to all forms of art, including literature. It forces the reader to question the possibility of ever being able to penetrate to the centre of the novel.

Place

The differences and similarities in the descriptions of the places in the novel call for analogous comparisons, the device on which the novel rests. The initial deliberately vague reference to the place where the story progresses arouses the reader's curiosity. The task of deciphering it is part of the ongoing scheme of detective work put upon the reader by the narration. Oren noted that the characters in all Tammuz's stories 'are walking in alleyways of Gentile cities and in foreign landscapes, and a dim familiar closeness is kindled within them'.[16] Alexander spends at some stage 12 years abroad, with only a few visits a year to Israel. (This is the same number of years that his father spent in the West, and the same number of years that Nikos travels around before arriving in Spain.) It is clear that at the opening of the story, the action takes place outside Israel. Several clues are given, such as the post from his family which is delivered to Alexander via an embassy, the lack of a permanent address and his stay in hotel rooms. Only at the very end of the first chapter, when the pharmacist quotes Shakespeare, does the reader realise that the action must be taking place outside Israel, possibly in England. Although Alexander is familiar with the country's customs, code of behaviour and institutions, he is an alien. (Indeed, the charm of the foreign woman, Jewish or not, is analogous to the charm of the western world: both Alexander's mother and Thea are foreign.) Superficially, the civilised afternoon tea taken on a summer afternoon in England is reminiscent of the equally civilised musical supper-parties given by Alexander's parents in Palestine, the similarity draws attention to the differences. In fact Thea's parents' flat in the comfortable part of town, with the noisy street and the coffee house opposite, stands in complete contrast with the isolated house in which Alexander grew up. Similarly, the continuous sound of the rush-hour traffic heard through the windows is as removed as can be from the sound of shooting guns which surrounds the house in the Jewish settlement.

The Near Eastern cities of Alexandria and the Lebanon are contrasted with European Germany where Nikos studies. Whilst the European changing seasons and the unfamiliar cherry and apple blossoms are undeniably beautiful, the sounds of the German language and the poetry which praises the beauty of the blue-eyed, white-skinned maidens whose looks he despises, are but a few of the warnings which eventually drive him away on his long journey to the south, or 'homewards', as he calls it. Like Alexander, he too is an alien, an alien in a country which has for him negative associations, including the menacing Nazi period:

> Every day from the library of the fourth floor he gazed at the line of trees on the horizon and saw how autumn advanced over the treetops, turning the fabric of the branches into transparent lace, behind which stretched the gloomy landscapes of eastern Europe. He knew that somewhere beyond the horizon lay Poland and then Russia and all those endless regions bearing Slavic names. Nikos would open the window and breathe in the chill air carried from the east and believe that he sensed in his nostrils the smell of smoke from distant chimneys, and heard a murmur of life all at once foreign, seductive, and menacing. A small voice, which had grown steadily more powerful in the course of a few months, started whispering to him, and then shouting and crying out to him, to pluck himself up by the roots and get out of there. (p.83, English edition)

This is juxtaposed with the contrasting description of the Lebanon:

> An eye-scorching summer sun poured out its light onto the harbour wall of the city of his childhood and melted the air that hopped, skipped, and jumped to the sound of thousands of peddlers, thousands of café record players, thousands of voices rising by semi-tones and trilling guttural songs. The aroma of the cardamom in the tiny cups of coffee, the smoke of hookahs bubbling up through jars of water wafted up and was lost in the sharp smell of roast lamb turning on charcoal and dripping its fat with a sizzling sound. (pp. 84–5, English edition)

This juxtaposition of the Near Eastern peoples with the Aryans made by Nikos is common to the Canaanite ideology to which Tammuz subscribed. The Canaanite movement saw the vast area of the 'Fertile Crescent' as having a common culture and hence as being one nation. This geo-historical philosophy, which believed in the natural territory absorbing into itself any ethnic group and digesting them into one 'nation of culture', was the foundation of the Canaanite doctrine. In his work on the subject, Shavit has pointed out that the Canaanites believed that

> there exists a mutual link between a certain 'geography' and the 'history' that occurs within it. Every human society, every civilization which is concentrated and consolidated within a specific territory as the result of various processes of settlement, migrations, conquests, and so forth, develops a view of the world from which are derived a specific and unique culture and values.[17]

In line with this ideology, Nikos believes that the Near Eastern countries share a common glorious past, which will be reawakened in the future. He explicitly evokes the memory of the Canaanite goddess Astarte as one of his ancestral matriarchs, thereby connecting his beliefs with Canaanite ideology (p.66). The Hebrew poet Yonatan Ratosh, the driving force behind the Canaanite movement, sought to revive Hebrew myths of gods and goddesses so that they could serve as the basis for a new Hebrew culture, parallel to the role of Greek myth in the shaping of European culture.[18] This aim is similar to the idea underlining Nikos's thesis which claims that similarities between peoples are based on their shared cultural values. Nikos believes that nothing will ever destroy the region which has survived for so many thousands of years:

> Jews, Hellenes, Muslims and Christians would come together and drift apart, slaughter one another and yearn for each other, and eventually leave the stage one after another. They would leave and return in cycles, in panic-stricken flight, with the sounds of calamity and destruction, the flash of warships going up in flames, the lamentation of mothers for their slain sons. And then there would be a prolonged silence, as if they were all rising from their graves and coming back in the smell of the roasting lamb, in the sound of the gramophones, in the tired, long, and despairing songs. (p.86, English edition)

It is the Greek songs which his sister used to sing in their child-hood that arouse Nikos's interest in the common traditions of the neighbouring Mediterranean peoples. He realises that they are all intermingled into one common culture: 'a well-mixed compound of a jumble of Jewish cantillation, Spanish flamenco, Neapolitan song, and some fragments from memory of the murmuring of a chorus from the ancient Greek tragedies' (pp.85–6, English edition). He traces the beginning of this process right back to the original songs of the Phoenician sailors, 'those ancients who had pulled the oars and unfurled the sails and had set out thousands of years ago from the very shore whose waves now licked the fringes of their garden' (p.86, English edition).

After his escape from decadent Europe, Alexander's father did not integrate in Palestine and refused to adapt himself to life in the new country. Whilst in Berlin he did absorb all that the place could offer, in Palestine he created a place which was separate and apart from its surroundings, regarding his neighbouring Jewish settlers as 'primitive' (p.90). Consequently, his life was a failure. Oren has pointed out (as noted earlier) that, like Brenner before him, Tammuz believed that only through pain can man preserve his passion for life.[19] The deepest pain of all is the pain of the uprooted, the exiled, which Tammuz portrayed in most of his writing. The protagonist of one of his short stories explained this:

> Of course I live for many and other reasons, but for this one too. And perhaps the most wonderful of all is the return home, the journey to the inner home that only the exiled and the uprooted know. And who is not an exile, who is not uprooted? Even people who live all their life in the country where they were born, even in the house in which they were born, they are exiles. . . . They do not know that they are exiles, but it makes no difference. . . . I will tell you something which might sound like a worthless philosophy, but that is your problem. . . . Listen: to my mind when a man is born – the moment he is born – he is uprooted and reaches the place of his exile. I seem to think that there is something like this in Jewish mysticism, that the soul descends from its original lofty abode . . . it descends. It is an interesting expression. And the soul comes to dwell on the earth, which is its exile. And all its days on the earth, the soul is longing for its place of origin. . . . Often the religious people express important ideas on these matters. . . . In other words: whoever is not uprooted from his place, is more of an exile than those who have been uprooted and who are at least aware of their condition and confront it. Does it not explain to you a little the secret of Jewish existence in exile?[20]

Places in Israel are portrayed with broad brushstrokes, evoking their historical and ideological background rather than their particular physical features. None of the places in Israel are mentioned by name. It is the history and ideology connected to the territory which concern Tammuz, and as such history is 'place'.[21] By contrast, cities abroad are mentioned by name (eventually), and they serve as an authentic setting for the plot. Only Berlin stands as a metaphor for a place which is the opposite of the Near East.

The conclusion that both Alexander and Nikos come to is that it is not the climate, the landscape, or the specific characteristics of the place which determine the character of the peoples, but rather the political and social circumstances dominating their lives. Alexander is the result of such circumstances. Despite the fact that his parents brought with them to the Near East their European cultural values, manners and a formed view of the world, their son absorbed very little of that. As a child, he spoke four languages (Russian, German, Hebrew and Arabic) and played the cello, yet he grows up to become the minotaur, a cross between a man and an animal. Unlike his parents, his vision necessitates violence and war as part of the process of redemption and progress. A shift in the Israeli takes place, from admiration of the spiritual values in life to admiration of the physical.

The heroic ethos has to be unencumbered by doubts and ethical restraints. This was one of the doctrines of the Canaanites,[22] and Tammuz suggests that, however ironic, this has also become a legitimate doctrine of the Israeli state establishment. The state creates creatures like the mythological minotaur. In the course of preserving the state, Alexander destroys those around him: his wife, his children, Thea, G. R. and Nikos. He is engaged to work for the very same establishment which only a few years back expelled him from school for his involvement with a politically right-wing splinter movement. The animal half of the minotaur represents the cruel, physical, aspect of Alexander's life, and the human half represents the aspirations for the spiritual. In contrast with his occupation, the human part of Alexander's monstrous character longs for love, and particularly for a love pure of sexuality. In one of his letters to Thea he explains:

> I chose this work because I have never loved anyone, except you, although all my life I have been trying to

love – in other words, to be unfaithful to you. I have
devoted my life to tough and disagreeable work
because I needed to love. And therefore I love the
country I serve, her mountains, her valleys, her dust
and despair, her roads and her paths. I acted as I did
through lack of choice. (p.6, English edition)

His love for the country is for him a substitute for a dream of a
love which can never be fulfilled.

NOTES

1. Including the one on the cover of the magazine *Minotaur*, published in
   1934. In the series of etchings entitled *Suite Vollard*, Picasso developed
   the subject of the minotaur. See Hans Bolliger, *Picasso's Vollard Suite*
   (London and New York: Thames and Hudson, 1987), p.xii.
2. Lael Wertenbaker, *The World of Picasso* (New York: Time Life, 1972),
   pp.105–6.
3. It has also been suggested that, in Jungian psychology, the minotaur
   embodies the irrational violence of the unconscious depths. Picasso represents the defeat of vulnerable, highly organised forces by the overwhelming forces of barbarism. He pictures the former in female symbols,
   and the latter in the male symbol of the bull-headed monster which
   draws its strength from the untamed depths of sexuality. See Wilhelm
   Boeck and Jaime Sabartes, *Pablo Picasso* (London: Thames and Hudson,
   1961), p.214.
4. As is well known, seven Athenian maidens and seven youths were regularly brought to Crete to be devoured by the minotaur, until it was killed
   by the Athenian hero Theseus, with the aid of Ariadne and her magic
   thread.
5. See Alex Preminger (ed.), *Poetry and Poetics* (New York: Macmillan
   Press, 1979), p.538.
6. *Hayei Elyakum (The Life of Elyakum)*, 1965; *Besof ma'arav (At the End
   of the West)*, 1966; and *Elyakum, sefer hahazayot (Elyakum, The Book
   of Hallucinations)*, 1969.
7. See, for example, pp.87, 108, 148. Unless otherwise noted, all page
   numbers in this chapter refer to the Hebrew text.
8. Compare, for example, the first version of Alexander's birthday at the
   opening of the novel with the second on p.136. Similarly, the first shooting scene on p.33 and the second on p.78, or the information regarding
   Thea's health given in the first version on p.80 and in the second on
   p.151, and so on.

9. Hereafter, when the English edition is mentioned, it refers to Kim Parfitt and Mildred Bundy's translation of *Minotaur* (London: Enigma Books, 1981).
10. For other self-referential comments see pp.13, 51, 148.
11. Abramov on p.84, Avram Abramov on p.85, Avram Alexandrovich on p.86.
12. For more on Alexander's complex relationship with the Arabs, see pp.90, 94, 110, 130–1, 133, 134-5.
13. Yosef Oren, *The Short Form in Israeli Narrative Fiction* (Rishon Letzion: Yahad, 1987), p.44.
14. See 'Hatzayar hale'umi shelanu' ('Our National Painter'), in *Reiho hamar shel hageranium (The Bitter Scent of Geranium)* (Tel Aviv: Hakibbutz Hameuchad, 1980), p. 70.
15. See pp.9–10 in this volume and n. 33.
16. Yosef Oren, *Hahitpakhut basiporet ha-Yisra'elit (Disillusionment in Israeli Narrative Fiction)* (Rishon Letzion: Yahad, 1983), p.47.
17. Yaacov Shavit, *The New Hebrew Nation: A Study in Heresy and Fantasy* (London: Frank Cass, 1987), pp.104–5.
18. See Yedidiah Yitshaki 'Iyun bashir "Haholchi vahoshech" – Yonatan Ratosh bein ha'ideolog lameshorer' ('A study of "Haholchi Vahoshech" – Yonatan Ratosh between ideologue and poet'), in *Hakevutza haCene'anit: sifrut veideologia (The Canaanite Group: Literature and Culture)* (The Open University, 1986), p.139. This anthology contains rich material on the Canaanites.
19. Yosef Oren, op. cit., p.44.
20. 'Beno shel Doctor Steinberg' ('Dr Steinberg's Son'), in *Reiho hamar shel hageranium (The Bitter Scent of Geranium)* (Tel Aviv: Hakibbutz Hameuchad, 1980), pp.175–6. In an interview Tammuz declared: 'All the other foreign places, which I love much more, are not mine, and do not facilitate anchorage. They are all just hotels, and despite all their initial attraction, they are tiresome and one has enough of them', *Hadoar,* n.d.
21. For the 'big place' see the Introduction, pp.7–8 in this volume.
22. Shavit pointed out that many saw the need to use violence and warfare as 'the distinct expression of the link between Canaanism and the nationalist, extremist right-wing ideologies burgeoning in Europe at that time', op. cit., p.126.

5

The Private Empire of Zmiri-Picasso

by SHLOMO NITZAN

This is a novel of conflicts: conflicts between father and son, between secular and religious Jews, and between Arabs and Israelis. These conflicts all contribute to the ongoing crisis of Israeli identity, at whose root lies the collective trauma of the Holocaust. Zmiri-Picasso, a Holocaust survivor, manages to build an empire in Israel, albeit an empire of paint and whitewash. His empire is successful despite the conflicts, all of which affect his life. However, because he lives in a dream, avoiding the conflicts and their causes, at the end his empire collapses on him. This is the alarming warning that Nitzan signals: 'You are all the captive of a dream, and in the meantime the dream has turned into a nightmare and no one has noticed' (p. 218). The analogy between the private empire and the State of Israel is transparent, and the novel should be read on these two levels.

Zmiri-Picasso is a middle-aged man, always too well dressed and laden with an expensive gold watch and heavy rings. His whole appearance is a statement of 'a considerable investment of large sums of money' (p.20) and of a man in authority. He is pleased with himself for having created something out of nothing, and is satisfied with the fact that he makes so much money. He arrived in Israel from the concentration camps with only the number tattooed on his arm, with his terrible memories and with the name Picasso, given to him in mockery by an educated German who saw him painting a fence in the camp. On his way to Israel he changed his name to a Hebrew one, Zmiri, trying symbolically but unsuccessfully to erase the horrors of his past. In fact, as a young boy he had wanted to become an artist, but through cruel history he becomes only the owner of a painting

97

and decorating company. Having survived, he is constantly pre-occupied with financial matters, has built a luxurious villa for his wife and son, and generously showers on his family all material comforts.

Nevertheless, his wife is never happy, never laughs, and feels like a captured bird, as her Yiddish name 'Feigele' indicates. She is Picasso's second wife, beautiful and, unlike his first wife (whom he divorced in Israel and with whom he had a daughter), much younger than himself. They met when she was working as a waitress in Jaffa, she too having just escaped the horrors of the concentration camp in Europe. Guessing the trauma in her life of which she never speaks, Picasso is incredibly patient with her, spoils her and tries to please her all the time. Yet she is always frightened and indifferent to his affection. She is left a mere shadow of herself, 'A corpse. Life ran away from her' (p.64). She feels permanently guilty because she alone from her well-to-do Hungarian family survived the Holocaust. To atone for that, she unnecessarily and obsessively cleans her house 'as if condemned for life to hard labour' (p.42), to clean away the past. She has no role other than, perhaps, to stand for all those who have been shattered.

Picasso is aware that Gavriel, their son, regards his mother as 'one who is not from here, one who does not belong' (p.49). He believes that Gavriel does not approve of him either, and blames himself for their failed relationship. His Hebrew is not good, he drinks a lot and is materialistically orientated – all of which is frowned upon by any typical Sabra such as his son. Then, too, the son does not quite match the image his father has of him (p.73). The father hopes that his son will want to do all the things that he was denied, and in his dominating manner he manages to dictate his son's development. As part of this scheme, Picasso wants his son to learn to drive before the permitted age. Gavriel has an accident with the result that he is confined to bed for a year, disturbing the normal course of growing up. His father's next wish is for him to become an officer in the army, an obsession which Batya, his daughter, explains: 'I only know that it is very important for him that his son should be an officer. Perhaps to prove something, to have revenge on someone. Perhaps the German officers' (p.171). The same motive must be behind his ownership of a large Doberman dog, to whom he speaks German, just as the German officers used to (p.45). These strong desires affect Gavriel so that whatever he does, wherever he is, he tries to please his father and act according to his expectations.

Thus, Gavriel's life is shaped by the constant shadow of his parents' Holocaust experience hanging over it. This phenomenon is not unique to Gavriel's family. For obvious reasons, the Holocaust experience was suppressed by most survivors, and we do not find it being expressed in post-war novels, in Hebrew or other languages. It is only since the 1960s that writers have become eager to confront the experience in their work. The Israeli author David Grossman has explained this development: 'For years, people had not talked about it. There were only secrets, only mythologies. I wanted to know how a human being, flesh and blood, would have coped . . . how I would have coped.'[1] However, although they try to hide any details from him, Picasso is disappointed that Gavriel never actually asks him about his past:

> Who am I to you, my son, what do you know about me except what I forced you sometimes to listen to, why don't you ask yourself, you never did ask. Why, Gavriel? Isn't it important for you to know, aren't you curious to know, you are satisfied with guesses? Well, guesses are also something. Somehow all of us guess one another, I too my late father, but sometimes one can guess not so correctly. Therefore, if possible it is better to ask. No? (pp.38–9)

He decides to send him to Germany where his brother Max lives, so that Gavriel can discover the family's roots which are 'scattered over several countries' (p.52). Gavriel does this, but in the process discovers other things as well, relating to his own identity. At the dramatic end of the novel, when Gavriel is accidentally wounded by a terrorist explosion whilst on the beach, he realises that he is going to die. He is the bound sacrifice, who is made to face all alone the unfair and unbearable burden put upon every young Israeli. There is no help from outside: 'Why don't they come, the army, the border militia, the police, the special unit, father, the Jewish people, Simon, Batya, mother, father, where are they all?' (p.210).

Through Max, the older and more educated of the two Zmiri brothers, Gavriel is exposed for the first time to an existential option which he did not know was possible. He is surprised to discover that Max does not have the need to belong to anything, and considers himself an individual free of religion and nationality. Israel for him is just 'another country' (p.95), and not necessarily the best solution of the problem for the Jews. Altogether he does not care much if there were no longer a Jewish people. He confesses to his astonished nephew:

> I simply find it difficult to understand the desire of the individual, not necessarily a Jew, but nowadays mainly Jews, this desire to belong, to live together, to give an expression to this desire in communal life. As if they are escaping to one another from a kind of catastrophe. How many tribes do you think there are in Africa? Well, I also don't know, but I imagine that there are many. Imagine that every tribe had insisted on living in a framework of its own nation state. We would then have had in the United Nations perhaps a thousand state members. Who needs this kind of mysticism? I, in any case, do not need it. I speak to you, my dear nephew, even though I do not expect your understanding. You are with them there in Israel; for you it is not even a matter of choice. For you it is a complete belonging, for life and death. And destiny. And war. Much war. In order to go much to war, there really needs to be a sense of belonging for life and death. In order to go much to war, perhaps it is forbidden to understand too many thoughts of others. Therefore, young man, I will not hold it against you at all if you don't listen to me. (p.97)

But Gavriel does listen, and it further confuses him about his identity, for he has already asked himself questions such as 'Who am I?', which hitherto had not even crossed his mind (p.93).

This crisis is part of a normal adolescence, but it is particularly pertinent because it happens on the eve of Gavriel being enlisted for three years in the Israeli army. On his return from Europe he spends a great deal of time discussing the army with his closest schoolfriends, Dorit and Micha. The prospect of serving for three whole years in the regular army, followed by 30 years of army reserve, is gloomy. In a banal and shallow conversation, the three friends discuss which unit is the best and the dangers of wars (pp.118–19). Woven into these talks is the complex relationship between the three. Gavriel loves Dorit, but was too shy to pursue a sexual relationship with her when they were still at school, and it is with Micha that she loses her virginity. Gavriel himself goes to a prostitute in Germany (p. 80), fulfilling his father's expectations, but thinking of Dorit all the time (in a scene which is repeated by the 'cheap' scene of Picasso's sex with a prostitute (p.140)).

Juxtaposed to this scene is a chapter which introduces the seedy characters of 'the second Israel', who frequent the hotel bar in the lower section of Haifa. There are two Arab visitors to the bar, both of whom come from the same village as the Arab waiter Othello. The presence of Arabs in the Jewish town and the tense relationships between them and the Israelis has already been introduced in the opening of the book and is one of the three main conflicts around which the story revolves. When the two decorators working for Picasso, one an Arab and the other a Jew, are accidentally left together in a locked room, the distrust and fear between them is unbearable, as the Jew reflects: 'the fear does not stop. It has its own logic, this fear. It is being nourished and it exists through the fear which is blowing from the Arab, like a bad smell' (p. 17). The Jew condemns the Arab for going out with a Jewish girl and, taking up a superior standpoint, blames him for being connected to recent terrorist incidents. The Arab does in fact have a relationship with an Israeli girl. He uses an Israeli name when he is introduced to her, and tries to take revenge for his miserable life by a sexual abuse. But his hatred turns to love (pp.31–2).

The two visitors at the hotel bar examine the place in a way which arouses the reader's suspicions as to their intentions.

Whilst extracting information about the owners of the place and its frequenters, the two Arabs humiliate Othello for working for Jews and make him feel a traitor to his own people:

> Othello, happy to serve them, hurried to bring them the freshest lamb 'shishlik specials' from behind the counter. Those which are not always ready in the fridge. And in his effort there was a great deal of willingness to please: the village, a kind of atonement for a sin which he had not committed, except for the sin of this job which is working for a Jew. (p.130)

Othello only guesses the purpose of their visit and his attempt to please them is mixed with hatred and anger at their invasion of his life. His fear comes true when on their second visit they pressurise him to collaborate with them, by evacuating the hotel bar for the night and placing an explosive at the crossroad.

It is Abed, the other Arab working at the bar as a dishwasher, who nurses a deep hatred of the Jews, counterbalancing the Jewish decorator's hatred of Arabs: 'Of course he hates them, if only he could not have done. This hatred of his does not harm them, but it chokes his throat. And then he gets angry and hates them even more. If there is a moment when he does not hate them he immediately thinks what happened, why?' (p.187). After the explosion on the beach, in which Gavriel and Dorit are accidentally wounded, the guard on duty thinks:

> That's it. Everything starts from here. He who comes to kill you, get up and kill him. True, true, not every Arab comes to kill. Every Arab is worthy a bullet. Every Arab has a dagger in his heart. Especially those from the territories, we don't need them here. They should go. Altogether it was not necessary to bring them here, let them stay there, in their territories, and the army should not let them move. They should be there, and we here, and that is it, peace . . . either they or us. (p.199)

Fear and hatred nourish the Arab–Israeli conflict, which is at the centre of Israeli life and of the novel.

The third central conflict is that between orthodox and secular Jews in Israel. Batya and Simon represent a certain kind of
orthodox Jew, who finds in religiosity a meaning to what otherwise would seem a pointless existence. In the novel, however,
the conversations between them and Gavriel and his shallow
thoughts about orthodoxy throw very little light on the subject's complexity. Batya marries Simon, who has left secular life
in England to become an ultra orthodox Jew in Jerusalem.
Although they do not break their relationship with their fami-
lies, they meet them only occasionally and their different ways
of life are unbridgeable: 'Picasso did not understand, did not
even begin or try to understand his daughter's decision. She in
her way in Jerusalem, and he in his here' (p.167). Gavriel is
more curious about Simon's conversion to orthodoxy, and sus-
pects that the newly found belief can only be seen as a kind of
cure for some sickness or weakness of Simon's. Otherwise he
cannot comprehend the change or believe in its sincerity – not
even when he himself wants to believe in something after he has
returned to Israel in a state of confusion from his visit to
Germany.

The novel is written in different speech registers, to match
the characters concerned: a lower, everyday, register (for example, pp.12, 14, 17); young Israelis' speech (for example, p.116);
Arabs' speech (for example, pp.133, 142, 151); and a higher
register for narration (for example, p.137). This is not an easy
undertaking since contemporary Hebrew has not yet developed
linguistic cultural and class distinctions. As a result, some of the
dialogues are forced and not always convincing in their authen-
ticity. In addition, the narration shifts unexpectedly from one
standpoint to another, including to the characters' inner
thoughts. Neither direct nor recorded speech is marked with
inverted commas, which obliterates the difference between the
two and adds to the confusion for the reader, who at first is not
certain whose voice is being heard. It is a device to keep the
reader constantly alert.

Place

The novel opens with a description of the view from the heights of a multi-storey building in Haifa, where two of Picasso's employees are working. Fear and threat are emphasised by a terrible and ominous silence. The tension between the Jew and the Arab is further symbolised by the spatial opposition created between the horizontal sea and the vertical mountains, which allure the two: 'Lutfi [the Arab], standing by the opening of the window which was gaping to the mountains, Mamus [the Jew] by the window which was gaping to the sea' (p.9). Yet, despite the differences, the mountains and the sea seem to offer the possibility of escape from the sense of urban claustrophobia, heavy heat and isolation shared by both. The town itself is also enclosed, ironically by the very same mountains and sea which suggest escape to the protagonists. It is only the open sky which hints at a possible real outlet. In a pattern of concentric circles, even the sea, in turn, is described as being imprisoned within distant shores, despite the illusion of its wide horizon: 'Just look at it, cast a glance and look at this terrible and wonderful sea of all times and of all generations. And also with all the colours, always here. Just pretends to be an innocent giant. . . . A jabbering innocent huge baby. An innocent baby imprisoned by such distant shores as one country is separated from another' (p.16). The sea, which is so dominant at the opening and the closing of the novel, becomes a particularly important feature of the landscape and is used not only in its literal but also various metaphorical meanings.

The two terrorists who are responsible for the tragedy at the end, look at the sea, towards other lands far beyond the horizon, and reach a conclusion: 'The sea which connects, is the very same sea which separates. And vice versa: the sea which separates, it too is the sea which connects' (p. 176). It separates and at the same time connects Israel and the European countries, as well as Israel and the Arab countries, all of which lie on the shores of the same Mediterranean sea. The only common denominator is their geographical location, but nevertheless it is common to all these Mediterranean peoples. Thus the Arabs

104

in the novel come to a conclusion similar to the Jewish Gavriel's: 'I belong to the Mediterranean' (p.93).

Picasso sends his son abroad to see Europe for the first time, to visit the town where he was born, as well as visiting his brother who lives in Germany. On his return Picasso expects his son 'to work, to live and to fight' (p.38), just as he has done. What he does not anticipate is that the visit would cast doubts in his son's mind about this expected way of life. Before the trip abroad, an alternative possibility of Jewish existence is unthinkable to Gavriel (for example, p.99). His uncle, who treats Israel only as one of many stations in his life, rather than an ultimate home for Jews, and his Jewishness only as a chance of birth, expresses some of these heretical ideas (pp.87, 95, 99). They are alien to Gavriel as they undoubtedly would be to any young Israeli brought up on Zionist ideology: 'a man is born in a place where he chooses to live now, not in a place where he was once born. Why should a place where others gave me birth, albeit my parents, be my place and not the place where I now live by my own free choice? . . . Don't you think so? Obviously you don't. You are an Israeli, so how can you understand?' (p. 87). Home, according to the uncle, can be wherever the individual chooses it to be, and Jewish existence is not bound to a particular territory such as the Jewish State (p. 99). These ideas shock Gavriel and force him to examine his views; eventually he concludes that he needs to live nowhere but in the State of Israel.

Initially, Gavriel enjoys travelling in beautiful countries abroad, released for the first time from the unusual sense of belonging to a place: 'It is for a release such as this that people travel from their own country to visit another country, isn't it? So as not to belong. To become passers-by even just for a short while in their life' (p. 87). This unfamiliar sensation seizes him only after he has fulfilled his obligation to his father by visiting Pietro Neimtz in Romania, his father's home town. The place holds such memories for his father that he cannot marshal enough courage to visit it himself. This is not just because of the usual fear for an adult of the reality destroying one's memories, but because of the associations of the place with the Holocaust. Normally, all the places of our past which remain with us are comforting, but not so for Holocaust survivors.[2] Picasso wants his son to see the place of his childhood, its sites, its river and its landscape (p.83). It seems to be a tragedy, but not a surprise, that Gavriel cannot identify himself with the alien landscape, so close to his father. In an imaginary dialogue with his father he confesses:

> Everything, including the scenery, was familiar to me from your stories. Having seen them all, they remained just as alien to me as they were before, when you told me about them. The river and the bridges, the trees, the foliage and the colourful fall and that special light reflected from the yellow-red bricks of the buildings. And the roofs of the houses and the chiming of church bells. Beautiful places, really. But why should all this become connected to me just because it was to you? (pp.85–6)

Even before he meets his uncle and hears his unsettling views about place, Gavriel is here questioning the expected connections to particular places.

The description of the scenery abroad stands in stark contrast to the scenery described in Israel. There is a sense of detachment with the first, and involvement, mainly political, with the second. In both, the places are described simply in realistic terms, but in the second the reader notices that the descriptions assume a metaphoric function. The sea in Israel is associated with terrorism, the mountains with the enemy, and the countryside with war memorials (p.56). Whilst the roads branching off the crossroads in Haifa are deserted, apparently leading to nowhere, the roads going away from the railway station in Hamburg lead to definite destinations in all parts of the world. It is at the railway station, far from home, that Gavriel searches for his own identity:

> the movement of all this huge traffic from the city's streets into the station, and from the station into all the passages underground, and the openings of all the

city's four corners, passes through my body, and crushed, I am being carried and swallowed up until I stop knowing who I am. . . . There I am, with my anxiety of losing the sense of my self-identity, within a terrible yet deep desire to lose it. To stand there in the middle of the tumult of the huge railway station, just like in the middle of the world, the middle of life, and suddenly ask: who am I? (p.93)

The author places his protagonist abroad, whence it is easier to raise these questions. Gavriel's travels serve to crystallise his feelings towards Israel, that he belongs there. In this respect, *Private Empire* is a reincarnation of the early Hebrew travelogues of the turn of the century, which also held dialogues with the Land, albeit from within. As Yaffa Berlovitz has summed it up: 'The travelogue, with all its changes and its different implications, is a story with an ongoing dialogue through which every generation tries to explain what this land means to it, and the meaning of belonging to this land.'³ Gavriel returns home with an unequivocal answer: 'I am not from here [Europe], I was born in the Middle East' (p.93). He cannot understand a Jew choosing to live outside Israel, even though he does not quite know what sort of a Jew he, as an Israeli, is (p.94). But, having returned home, he is restless, as his girlfriend Dorit observes: 'When you are there, you want in the middle of it all to return home. Having only just arrived back, you want to return there. This is exactly what you are, wanting always to be in a place where you are not' (p.114). Gavriel's odyssey in search of his identity as a Jew and as an Israeli ends with his cruel death. Nitzan leads us to believe that this would not have been the case had he survived. Though historical forces drive him to believe in, and die for, the necessity of belonging to one territorial homeland, the wandering spirit of the Wandering Jew would have persisted to disquieten his existence. Like that mythical hero, Gavriel goes through the first two phases of a journey – the setting out and the trials of adventure – but, unlike him, on his return Gavriel is not given the chance to reintegrate into society.

NOTES

1. David Grossman, 'Perpetual Redemption: David Grossman's "See Under Love"', *Jewish Quarterly* (Spring 1990), p.17.
2. For a systematic study of the sites of our intimate life see Gaston Bachelard, *The Poetics of Space* (Boston: Beacon Press, 1969), pp.9–10.
3. Yaffa Berlovitz, *E'ebra na ba'aretz* (*Wandering in the Land*) (Tel Aviv: Misrad Habitahon, 1992), p.371.

6

Not of This Time, Not of This Place

by YEHUDA AMICHAI

The theme of home and abroad is presented in a most unusual and original form in Amichai's rich and expansive novel, *Not of This Time, Not of This Place*, published as early as 1963. By using this theme at that time he was breaking the poetic norm, something which is evident in all other aspects of his writings. Amichai can be regarded as a precursor of the group of writers of the 1980s, and as such it seems fit to conclude this study with just a brief analysis of this text.

Amichai's novel *Not of This Time, Not of This Place*[1] intro-duces the poetic uses of the fantastic, and explores its unex-pected literary possibilities when applying the dialectics of home and abroad. Amichai placed Joel, the novel's protagonist who is in his late thirties, in two different geographical loca-tions simultaneously. Jerusalem and Bavarian Weinburg are the two juxtaposed cities where the two parallel stories of Joel's life simultaneously take place, representing two aspects of his char-acter. The two parallel stories, which are marked with surreal elements, are significantly presented from two different view-points: the story of Joel in Jerusalem is narrated in the third person whereas the story of Joel in Weinburg is narrated in the first person. This emphasises the psychological split in Joel's life, where Jerusalem belongs to the present and Weinburg belongs to his past. The two are irreconcilable parts of his per-sonality. Yet, they constitute not only Joel's personal biography, but that of a whole generation which survived Nazi Germany. Although his voice is the voice of the individual, it is a voice which cannot disassociate itself from the collective: 'I stood there and I cried within myself about the destruction of my life and the destruction of Jerusalem' (p.52).[2] In this novel Amichai emphasises that man is never on his own but is always part of the whole generation, and that the two are intertwined (for example, pp.416, 597, 607).

Significantly, Joel is an archaeologist whose aim is to unearth the mysteries of the past. The linking in the story between the earth, or the place, and the past is based not so much on some hidden resemblance or analogy between the Time and the Place of the novel's title, but rather on external relation, and thus the place functions as a metonym for the long history of Israel. The Biblical period, the Second Temple, the Roman and the Crusaders' invasion, the long wars between Jew and Arab, have all left their mark as layers of the very earth which Joel has been excavating. In addition, the ever presence of a no-man's land which has split the city into two is a constant reminder of the blood spilt by man in futile wars as well as creating a sense of an inescapable siege. Joel was attracted to the no-man's land, that dangerous area which receives special mention throughout the story, and which is where he and Mina eventually meet their deaths (for example, pp.147, 157, 471, 500–1). It was an area saturated with the blood of many generations (for example, pp.28, 90). Jerusalem and its history, Place and Time, are thus seen as full of blood and destruction, and even the onslaught of the summer is perceived by Joel as the arriving armies of Titus and Nebuchadnezzar (p.141). It is a hard, stony city (for example, pp.220, 571), dried up and full of despair, cemeteries, funerals and death (pp.263, 325, 377). Nevertheless, after each destruction a new era emerges (p.550). Contemporary Jerusalem, with its different houses and neighbourhoods (for example, pp.26–7, 36, 91–2, 105, 114, 115, 169, 498–9, 502, 604), the sensuous smells of its trees (for example, pp.7, 101) and its mesmerising fascination, is a place pulsating with life. The native born and immigrants, the cultured and the uncultured, orientals and occidentals, Jews, Christians and Moslems, all create a colourful, if complex, tapestry of daily life.

Set against Jerusalem, the parallel plot of the story takes place in Weinburg. The comparison of the two cities serves as a poetic tool in the structure of the novel. This is but one of countless apparent analogies upon which the story rests, as pointed out by Gershon Shaked in his analysis of the story.[3] I would like to argue that the endless analogies in the story are not its weakness, but its strength, and that they have a similar fuction to that of the analogy which binds the different units of his poems. Amichai is teasing the reader with suggestions and hints of analogies, but in the final analysis they do not all hold their ground. There is no analogy between Jerusalem and Weinburg, any more than there is between the Holocaust and other catastrophic events in history.

The strange, irrational idea of going back to Germany and yet of remaining in Jerusalem at the same time was suggested to Joel by his psychiatrically sick friend Mina, a Holocaust survivor. The purpose of going back to Weinburg was to take revenge for Ruth, his childhood girlfriend, who perished in the concentration camps. Bearing in mind the strong autobiographical aspect of Amichai's prose and poetry, Joel's journey thus assumes an added dimension. His journey abroad serves a very specific function: this is not just the case of the protagonist asking questions about himself and about the nature of the whole Israeli enterprise when placed abroad, but it is also the case of him confronting particularly the memory of the Holocaust. He thought that revenge would cure his sorrows, and the importance of revenge in the scheme of events is indicated by the motto of the novel: 'He saw a skull floating on the waters and he said to it: because you have caused others to drown, you will drown, and those who caused you to drown will ultimately also drown' (Pirkei Avot B, p.6; also pp.156, 157, 277, 364, 422, 518, 533, 541, 550, 552, 584, 592, 612). However, Joel discovered that erasing memories of terrible events is a better and more effective cure. The way forward in life is to be able to forget. On his journey abroad, Joel stayed in Zurich for a few days. He needed to detach himself from Jerusalem and to get used to the thought of being in a German-speaking country once again (p.53). Similarly, he needed a few days in Paris on his way back home to Jerusalem. But, above all, it is Weinburg which creates the dialectics of home and abroad, inside and outside, discussed in my Introduction.

111

Weinburg is a city with a river, bridges and fountains (pp.153, 155, 174, 175), in contrast to Jerusalem which is dry. Like Jerusalem it is stony, but here the stone indicates civilisation, not destruction: the stone has been made into carvings, statues and sculptures of angelic and saintly figures and of medieval heroes (for example, p.560). The irony is that it is in this seemingly cultured city that Jews were so savagely murdered (pp.580-1). Although there is some evidence of destruction in Weinburg, most of the city was completely rebuilt after the war (for example, pp.105, 153, 180) and it has remained the city of towers, churches (for example, pp.97-8, 149) and wine cellars it always was. Whilst parts of Jerusalem have also been rebuilt, the evidence of the past could never be erased there. Joel was excited to see again the familiar landscape of his childhood and enjoyed the natural beauty of the surroundings of Weinburg (pp.76, 86, 492). Sentimental memories and childhood attachments intermittently obscured his hatred for the place. His visit to Bachfeld, his late grandparents' village, further emphasises his ambiguous love–hate feelings towards Germany. The familiar landscape had not changed here despite the terrible war, and the destruction did not leave its mark in the earth for an archaeologist to discover.

The story set in Jerusalem is the account of Joel's sensuous love for a strange Christian woman. His love helps him escape the conventions of family framework and social expectations. The end of the relationship seems to illustrate that it is possible for love to leave no traces. The story set in Weinburg is the account of Joel's journey for revenge and it appears to illustrate that, unlike love, war and revenge do leave traces. However, typical to many of Amichai's teasing analogies in this novel, love and revenge are, ironically, no different from one another: both leave traces. It seems interesting to note the close relationship between Amichai's prose and poetry, which can be exemplified in this particular case by one of Amichai's poems. In 'The Travels of the Last Benjamin of Tudela', the speaker announces:

> Come, my bride, in your hand hold something made of clay
> At sunset, for flesh melts away

And iron is not preserved. Hold clay in your hand,
So that future archaeologists should find and remember.
They know not that even anemones, after the rain
Are an archaeological find and a great attestation.[4]

The poem contains many poetic and thematic elements which have been transferred from Amichai's poetry and extended further in his prose.

Through Joel's endless wanderings in all parts of Weinburg in search of his childhood, he records the minute details of buildings and neighbourhoods in the town. The accumulative effect is achieved through the use of the 'catalogue' technique, discussed at length by Boaz Arpali in his book about Amichai's poetry.[5] Joel was particularly attracted to the central railway station, which epitomises the 'big voyage' mentioned in my Introduction. 'A railway station is the native land of wanderers the world over. Railway stations are the embassies of all the homeless, or of those who have left their homes by choice and are in a state of complete oblivion. This is comparable to the "big voyage"' (p.96). As already mentioned in my Introduction, many leading twentieth-century authors write about the journey as a temporary solution for their protagonists in their search for their place in the world. This coincides with the state of mind of modern humanity, which has lost its sense of belonging. We find that the idea of place has become empty and our modern consciousness has become a 'homeless mind', never quite finding its place. This is the case for Amichai's protagonist (for example, pp.278, 345, 489). His version of the 'big voyage' is being compared to Lot's wife, turned into a stationary pillar of salt yet always trying to run away (p.549). Similar to the 'secular pilgrim' already mentioned,[6] Joel too is in a state of unrest, of constant movement.

Joel's problems are specific to a Holocaust survivor, but at the same time they also represent some of the problems of modern human consciousness. The dialectics of home and abroad are an interesting poetic device through which Amichai chose to convey these problems. Joel's endless and often meaningless wanderings are a warped reincarnation of the Odyssean epic.

They often involve pain and suffering, but they also involve promise, hope and renewal, as is the case in the novel. Joel missed home and began his big journey back commenting: 'When one is away from home, home hurts like a tooth; as if home is part of one's body' (p.462).

Joel's process of personal and collective reconciliation and renewal had begun to take place. He left Jerusalem, yet wanted to return (pp.496, 584, 618), reflecting: 'I suddenly understood why God is called the Place' (p.591). This idea refers to the Bible's attitude towards wandering, which is seen as a movement towards the right place, towards God who Himself is subsequently referred to as 'the Place'.[7] However, unlike the wanderings of modernist protagonists who are in search of their personal solutions, Joel's are also in search of solutions for the collective (p.272) which is one of the distinguishing features of contemporary Israeli literature. Through the dialectics of home and abroad, inside and outside, Amichai's protagonist could confront his past so that he would be able to live the present. A certain degree of harmony could only be gained when the memory of his past had been confronted, and when the tension between home and abroad has been clearly defined, yet diffused. To achieve this, his protagonist had to travel far in order to say: 'this reminds me of another place'.

NOTES

1. Y. Amichai, *Lo me'achshav lo mikan (Not of This Time, Not of This Place)* (Jerusalem and Tel Aviv: Schocken, 1975 (second edition)).

2. All translations are my own, and are literal rather than literary. I could not rely on the English translation of the book by Shlomo Katz (London: Vallentine Mitchell, 1973), since it has been heavily edited.

3. 'Hor dor i he'atzuv vehamukeh' ('Woe to My Sad and Stricken Generation'), in *Yehuda Amichai, mivhar ma'amarei bikkoret 'al vetsirato (Yehuda Amichai – A selection of critical essays on his writing)*, selected and introduced by Y. Tzvik (Tel Aviv: Hakibbutz Hameuchad, 1988), pp.191-213.

4. Y. Amichai, *Achshav ba-ra'ash (Now, in the Midst of the Noise)* (Jerusalem and Tel Aviv: Schocken, 1968), p.129.

5. Boaz Arpali, *Haprahim ve-ha'agratal, shirat Amichai 1948–1968 (mivneh, mashma'oot, politica) (The flowers and the urn – Amihai's poetry 1948–1968 (Structure, Meaning, Poetics))* (Tel Aviv: Hakibbutz Hameuchad, 1986).

6. See my Introduction.

7. Ibid.

Bibliography

Books

Mediterranean Historical Review (London: Frank Cass).

Mediterranean Language Review (Wiesbaden: Harrassowitz Verlag).

Agnon, S.Y., 'Ido ve-Inam' ('Ido and Inam'), *Ad Henah (Unto Here)* (Tel Aviv: Schocken, 1971).

Almog, Ruth, *Mavet bageshem (Death in the Rain)* (Jerusalem: Keter Publishing House, 1982), trans. Dalya Bilu, *Death in the Rain* (Santa Fe, New Mexico: Red Crane books, 1993).

Alter, Robert, 'Afterword: A Problem of Horizons', in E. Anderson (ed.), *Contemporary Israeli Literature* (Philadelphia: Jewish Publication Society of America, 1977).

Amichai, Yehuda, *Me'ahorei kol zeh mistater osher gadol (Behind All This Hides Great Happiness)* (Jerusalem and Tel Aviv: Schocken, 1974).

— *Lo me'achshav lo mikan (Not of This Time, Not of This Place)* (Jerusalem and Tel Aviv: Schocken, 1975).

Bachelard, Gaston, *The Poetics of Space* (Boston: Beacon Press, 1969).

Balaban, A., *Mar Molcho (Mr Molcho)* (Tel Aviv: Hakibbutz Hameuchad, n.d.).

Bartana, Ortsion, *Lavo heshbon (To Call to Account)* (Tel Aviv: Alef, 1985).

— *Shmonim (The Eighties)* (Tel Aviv: Agudat Hasofrim, 1993).

— *Zehirut, sifrut Eretz-Yisra'eli (Caution, Israeli Literature)* (Papyrus, 1989).

Berlovitz, Yaffa, *E'ebra na ba'aretz (Wandering in the Land)* (Tel Aviv: Misrad Habitahon, 1992).

Boeck, Wilhelm and Sabartes, Jaime, *Pablo Picasso* (London: Thames and Hudson, 1961).

Bolliger, Hans, *Picasso's Vollard Suite* (London and New York: Thames and Hudson, 1987).

Bowie, Malcolm, *Freud, Proust and Lacan: Theory as Fiction* (Cambridge University Press, 1988).

Brenner, Y.H., *Atzabim (Nerves)* (Tel Aviv: Hakibbutz Hameuchad, 1956).

Broe, Mary Lynn, and Ingram, Angela (eds), *Women's Writing in Exile* (Chapel Hill and London: University of North Carolina, 1981).

Calderon, Nissim, *Hargasha shel makom (A Sense of Place)* (Tel Aviv: Hakibbutz Hameuchad, 1988).

Cohen, Joseph, *Voices of Israel* (State University of New York Press, 1990).

Culler, Johnathan, *The Pursuit of Signs* (London: Routledge & Kegan Paul, 1983).

Friedman, Susan Stanford, 'Exile in the American Grain', in Mary Lynn Broe and Angela Ingrams (eds), *Women's Writing in Exile* (Chapel Hill and London: University of North Carolina, 1989).

Fussell, Paul, *Abroad: British Literary Travelling Between the Wars* (New York: Oxford University Press, 1990).

Gilboa, Menucha, 'America kemakom, kemetaphora ukesemel bishlosha romanim' ('America as a place, a metaphor and a symbol in three novels'), in Stanley Nash (ed.), *Migvan* (Lod: Habberman Institute for Research in Literature, 1988).

Govrin, Nurit, 'Yerushalayim ve-Tel Aviv kemetaphorot basifrut ha'ivrit hitpathuta shel tadmit' ('Jerusalem and Tel Aviv as Metaphors in Hebrew Literature: Development of an Image'), *Yerushalayim batoda'ah uva'asiyah hatzionit (Jerusalem in Zionist Consciousness and Action)* (Jerusalem: Hebrew University, 1989).

Hawking, Stephen W., *A Brief History of Time* (London: Bantam, 1988).

Iser, Wolfgang, *The Act of Reading: A Theory of Aesthetic Response* (London: Routledge & Kegan Paul, 1978).

— 'The Reading Process: A Phenomenological Approach', in Jane P. Tompkins (ed.), *Reader-Response: From Formalism to Post-Structuralism* (Baltimore and London: John Hopkins University Press, 1981).

Kurtzweil, B., *Sifrutenu hahadasha; hemshech o mahapecha (Our New Literature: Continuation or Revolution)* (Jerusalem and Tel Aviv: Schocken, 1959).

Lodge, David, *Working with Structuralism* (London: Routledge & Kegan Paul, 1981).

— *After Bakhtin: Essays on Fiction and Criticism* (London: Routledge, 1990).

Mintz, Alan, *'Banished From Their Father's Table': Loss of Faith and Hebrew Autobiography* (Bloomington: Indiana University Press, 1989).

Miron, Dan, *Im lo tiheye Yerushalayim (If There is no Jerusalem)* (Tel Aviv: Hakibbutz Hameuchad, 1987).

Nitzan, Shlomo, *Ha'imperia hapratit shel Zmiri-Picasso (The Private Empire of Zimri-Picasso)* (Tel Aviv: Sifriyat Hapoalim, 1982).

Oren, Yithak, *Hatzda'ah lasifrut ha-Yisra'elit (Salute to Israeli Literature)* (Rishon Letzion: Yahad, 1991).

Oren, Yosef, *Hahitpakhut basiporet ha-Yisra'elit (Disillusionment in Israeli Narrative Fiction)* (Rishon Letzion: Yahad, 1983).

— *The Short Form in Israeli Narrative Fiction* (Rishon Letzion: Yahad, 1987).

— *Tziyonut vetzabariyut baroman ha-Yisra'eli (Zionism and Sabraism in the Israeli Novel)* (Rishon Letzion: Yahad, 1990).

Orpaz, Yithak, *Hatzalian hahiloni (The Secular Pilgrim)* (Tel Aviv: Hakibbutz Hameuchad, 1982).

Preminger, Alex (ed.), *Poetry and Poetics* (New York: Macmillan Press, 1979).

Rimmon-Kenan, Shlomith, *Narrative Fiction: Contemporary Poetics* (London: Methuen, 1983).

Rubinstein, Amnon, *Liheyot am hofshi (To Be a Free People)* (Jerusalem and Tel Aviv: Schocken, 1977).

Runes, Dagobert D. (ed.), *Dictionary of Philosophy* (London: Peter Owen, 1972).

BIBLIOGRAPHY

Searle, John, 'Metaphor', in Andrew Ortony (ed.), *Metaphor and Thought* (Cambridge University Press, 1981).

Selden, Raman, *Reader's Guide to Contemporary Literary Theory* (London: Harvester Press, 1988).

Shabtai, Edna, *Vaharei 'at (For Love is Strong as Death)* (Jerusalem: Keter, 1986).

Shabtai, Yaakov, *Sof davar* (Tel Aviv: Siman Kriah/Hakibbutz Hameuchad, 1984), trans. Dalya Bilu, *Past Perfect* (New York: Viking Penguin, 1987).

Shaked, Gershon, *Lelo motza (Dead End)* (Tel Aviv: Hakibbutz Hameuchad, 1973).

— 'Challenges and Question Marks: On the Political Meaning of Hebrew Fiction in the Seventies and Eighties', *P.E.N. Israel, 1991, A Collection of Recent Writing in Israel* (Ramat Gan: Institute for the Translation of Hebrew Literature, 1991).

Shapira, Sarit, *Maslulei nedudim (Routes of Wandering)*, exh. cat., The Israel Museum (Jerusalem, 1991).

Shavit, Yaakov, *The New Hebrew Nation: A Study in Heresy and Fantasy* (London: Frank Cass, 1987).

— *Hayahadut bir'ee hayavnut (Judaism in the Greek Mirror and the Emergence of the Modern Hellenised Jew)* (Tel Aviv: Am Oved, 1992).

Sontag, Susan, *Illness as Metaphor* (London: Allen Lane, 1978).

Tammuz, Benjamin, *Minotaur* (Tel Aviv: Hakibbutz Hameuchad, 1980), trans. Kim Parfitt and Mildred Bundy (London: Enigma Books, 1981).

— 'Hatzayar hale'umi shelanu' ('Our National Painter') and 'Beno shel Doctor Steinberg' ('Doctor Steinberg's Son'), in *Reiho hamar shel hageranium (The Bitter Scent of Geranium)* (Tel Aviv: Hakibbutz Hameuchad, 1980).

Waugh, Patricia, *Metafiction* (London: Methuen, 1984).

Wellek, René and Warren, Austin, *Theory of Literature* (Harmondsworth: Penguin Books, 1973).

Wertenbaker, Lael, *The World of Picasso* (New York: Time-Life, 1972).

Yehoshua, A.B., *Molcho* (Tel Aviv: Hakibbutz Hameuchad, 1987), Eng., *Five Seasons* (London: Flamingo, 1990).

Yitshaki, Yedidiah, 'Iyun bashir "Haholchi vahoshech" – Yonatan Ratosh bein ha'ideolog lameshorer' ('A Study of "Haholchi Vahoshech" – Yonatan Ratosh between ideologue and poet'), in *Hakevutza haKene'anit: sifrut veideologia (The Canaanite Group: Literature and Culture)* (The Open University, 1986).

Zach, Nathan, 'Hamasa hagadol' ('The Big Voyage'), *Igra, Almanac for Literature and Art* (Jerusalem: Carmel, 1990).

Articles

Aran, David, 'Od kama he'arot al "Molcho"' ('More Comments on "Molcho"'), *Al Hamishmar*, 5 June 1988.

117

Bartana, Ortsion, 'Sipur marshim umefutzal' ('An Impressive and Diverse Story'), *Davar*, 6 March 1987.

Bronowsky, Yoram, 'Yam tichoniyut, eich?' ('Mediterranean, How?'), *Ha-Aretz*, 12 Oct. 1990.

Derrida, Jacques, 'Structure, Sign, and Play' (1966), in Susan Handelman, 'Parodic Play and Prophetic Reason: Two Interpretations of Interpretation', *Poetics Today* (Durham, NC: Duke University Press), Vol. 9, No. 2 (1988).

Geldman, M., 'Maslulei nedudim' ('Routes of Wandering'), *Ah'shav* 58 (Spring/Summer 1992).

Grossman, David, 'Perpetual Redemption: David Grossman's "See Under Love"', *The Jewish Quarterly* (Spring 1990).

Gurevich, Zali, and Aran, Gideon, 'Al hamakom (Antropologia Yisra'elite)' ('About the Place (Israeli Anthropology)'), *Alpayim* 4 (1991).

Hagorni-Green, Abraham, 'Sipporet bat yameinu' ('Contemporary Hebrew Narrative'), *Or-Am* (1989).

Hopp, Doreet, 'Molcho bashe'ol' ('Molcho in the Underworld'), *Siman Keri'ah*, Vol. 20 (May 1990).

Kimmerling, Baruch, 'Al da'at hamakom' ('On the use of the term "place" as a surrogate for deity'), *Alpayim* 6 (1992).

Laor, Dan, 'Bein hametim uvein hahayim' ('Between the Living and the Dead'), *Ha-Aretz*, 27 Feb. 1987.

Laor, Yitzhak, 'Kotvim et ha'aretz' ('Writing the Country'), *Ha-Aretz*, 31 Jan. 1992.

Levy, Itamar, 'Le'an nodedim hanedudim' ('Where do wanderings wander?'), *Ha-Aretz*, 6 March 1992.

— 'Hayehudi hamudhak' ('The Suppressed Jew'), *Ha-Aretz*, 13 March 1992.

Link, Baruch, 'Liheyot Italki!...Liheyo meshorer!' ('To be Italian!...To be a poet!'), *Alei siach* 26 (Tel Aviv: Hachugim Lesifrut, 1989).

Meroz, T., 'Tamar Meroz interviews Edna Shabtai', in *Modern Hebrew Literature* (Institute for Translation of Hebrew Literature), 3:4 (Spring/Summer 1985), Vol. 10.

Ne'eman, Michal, 'Ma nish'ar la'asot?' ('What is there left to do?'), *Yediot Aharonot,* 13 April 1987.

Oryan, Yehudit, 'Lehamit be'ahava' ('To Kill with Love'), *Yediot Aharonot,* 6 Feb. 1987.

Shabtai, Edna, 'Tel Aviv baprosa shel Ya'akov Shabtai' ('Tel Aviv in the prose of Yaakov Shabtai'), *Ahi'shav* 56 (Spring/ Summer 1991).

Shaked, Gershon, 'Besof ma'arav' ('At the End of the West'), *Hadoar* (31 Oct. 1986), LXV: 40 (2831).

Shifra, Sh., 'Zara bimkoma' ('Stranger in her own Place'), *Yediot Aharanot,* 27 Nov. 1987.

Tanner, Tony, 'Additions to the World', *The Times Literary Supplement,* 14 Aug. 1992.

Taylor, John, 'Painless Progress', *The Times Literary Supplement,* 25 Sept. 1991.

BIBLIOGRAPHY

Werses, Prof. Shmuel, 'The Houses of Berdichevsky', *Mehkarei Yerushalayim basifrut (Jerusalem Studies in Hebrew),* No.5 (1984).

Yehoshua, A.B., 'Avraham B. Yehoshua', *Ma'ariv,* 28 June 1991.

— interview in *Ma'ariv,* 30 Jan. 1987 with Sarit Fuchs.

— report in *Ha'ir,* 20 March 1987.

Index

INDEX

INDEX